The Problem of Religious Knowledge

WILLIAM T. BLACKSTONE

The Problem of Religious Knowledge

The Impact of Philosophical Analysis on the Question of Religious Knowledge

Prentice-Hall, Inc. *Englewood Cliffs, N.J.*
A SPECTRUM BOOK

Englewood Cliffs, N.J.

Library of Congress Catalog No.: 63-11783

Printed in the United States of America

C

To my wife,
Jean

Preface

All human beings who have been inculcated with some religious perspective (and most of us have) are interested in the philosophical question of whether there is religious knowledge. This interest has had a tremendous revival in recent years. One can only speculate on the causes. Certainly the constant threat of the total destruction of human civilization by nuclear holocaust has been a factor. In view of such consequences, many have been motivated to rethink the philosophical-religious issues about the nature and destiny of man. Another factor responsible for the resurgence of interest in theological-religious issues, specifically among philosophers and students of philosophy, has been the development of new methods of analysis or a new approach to the meaning of "meaning." The inadequacy and arbitrariness of the positivist's rejection of religious and theological claims as meaningless is now generally recognized, and philosophers are busy re-examining theological-religious discourse with a new set of tools. There is a great deal of concern among alert students and educated laymen over this re-examination. They are puzzled about this new analysis and the implications it has for the logical status of religious beliefs.

This book is designed for those who have this concern and puzzlement (though, of course, it offers no guarantee of resolving such puzzlement). It is not designed to be a highly specialized and technical treatise in philosophy of religion but one which can be read and appreciated by students and educated laymen. It has two specific purposes, that of providing a clear picture of developments in contemporary philosophy and the impact of these developments in philosophy of religion, and that of systematically exploring the question, "Is there religious knowledge?" Contemporary philosophy is used as a point of reference for devising a framework within which this question can be answered. Space limitations have forced an all-too-brief treatment of some positions. Such brevity tends to distort but I have made efforts to avoid such distortion.

No particular religious viewpoint is imposed on the reader. The book is neutral in that respect, but it does take a clear stand on the methodological procedures for answering this important question and presents certain conclusions drawn by the author. It is hoped that this volume will fill a real gap in philosophical literature in the area of religion and that student and layman alike will derive benefit from it. It is also hoped that it will be of interest to the professional philosopher, particularly the treatment of the cognitive significance of religious claims and the critical analyses of the accounts of religion held by a number of contemporary philosophical analysts.

W.T.B.

Acknowledgments

I wish to acknowledge my debt to the following publishers who have kindly given permission to quote from their materials: Dover Publications, Inc., Princeton University Press, Routledge & Kegan Paul, Ltd., Westminster Press, University of Chicago Press, John Wiley & Sons, Inc., Harper and Row, Publishers, Basil Blackwell & Mott, Ltd., Prentice-Hall, Inc., Appleton-Century-Crofts, Inc., Student Christian Movement Press, Ltd., Philosophical Library, Inc., New York University Press, Longmans, Green and Co., Cornell University Press, The Clarendon Press, C. A. Watts and Co., Ltd., Cambridge University Press, Basic Books, Inc., Abingdon Press, James Clarke & Co., Ltd. and Penguin Books, Inc. Special acknowledgment is due the journals, *The Personalist* and *The Iliff Review,* for their permission to use material of mine that first appeared in these journals in article form, the General Research Office of the University of Georgia for financial aid in retyping the manuscript, and the University of Georgia for research time. I am also indebted to my colleagues in the Department of Philosophy and Religion at the University of Georgia for the help I received in discussion with them, and to Professors Reynolds of Elon College, Bowden of the Indiana School of Religion, Nielsen of New York University, Patterson and Peach of Duke University for early help and encouragement in dealing with the problems with which this study is concerned. My greatest debt is to my wife, Jean, who not only cheerfully typed the manuscript from my handwritten pages but also offered encouragement at just the right times.

Table of Contents

The Problem of Religious Knowledge

CHAPTER ONE

Introduction

Contemporary philosophy is distinguished from philosophy in the past by its intense concern with language and meaning. To be sure, this concern has taken different forms. The logical positivists offered one account of the meaning of "meaning" and one program for clarifying language. The philosophical analysts, under the influence of the Wittgenstein of the *Philosophical Investigations,* offer a different account and a different program. Philosophers in both these traditions have analyzed and attempted to clarify a number of areas of discourse—the languages of ethics, politics, science, metaphysics, and aesthetics. Recently, the language of religion and theology has undergone considerable analysis. The positivists, of course, had earlier written off religion and theology as being in large part factually meaningless, or noncognitive. More recent philosophical analysts, however, have introduced new and challenging discussions which emphasize a careful analysis of the uses or functions of religious concepts and statements in the context of their use. Both the logical positivists and the analysts who follow the later Wittgenstein agree that there are many uses of words in religious discourse which purport to communicate information but which do not, uses of words which are *misuses* or which really convey only nonsense. The problem for these analysts is that of formulating a way of deciding whether a particular use of words is proper or not, and whether it has factual significance or not. Many have applied their tools to the language of religion and have come up with interesting and often startling conclusions.

Although problems about the meaning of religious discourse have recently drawn intensive attention, these problems, of course, are ancient. When religious language was largely anthropomorphic, so that God or the religious object was described in terms derived from our experience (the God of parts of the Old Testament, for example), there was no problem concerning the meaning of religious language. God was viewed as a kind of superhuman being. When, however, theologians developed the concept of God as transcendent —as utterly beyond the world of our experience—it was questioned whether any predicates at all could be applied to God. If our ordinary predicates cannot be applied to God, how can we meaningfully talk about Him? Some philosophers and theologians straightforwardly stated that we cannot, at least that we cannot positively characterize Him. All we can do is say what God is not.

In spite of the fact that this conception of God generated numerous problems concerning the meaning of theological language, a number of religious thinkers found this transcendent conception of God advantageous. It precluded any attack from science, and it presumably did more honor to God by placing Him beyond any human conception. (In actual practice within Christianity, however, the anthropomorphism was brought in the back door, with talk about the life and teachings of Christ often taking the place of talk about God.) This transcendent view, many held, had the further advantage of teaching us that in religion "we must live by faith."

This latter contention, that religion is a matter of faith, deserves special mention. This reply misses the whole point of the analyst's question. In requesting the meaning of religious claims, the analyst is really asking what one is to have faith in. Can one urge someone to accept a belief or set of beliefs if the content of the belief or set of beliefs is not made clear? Surely not. Until the content of a belief is made clear, the appeal to accept the belief on faith is beside the point, for one would not know what one has accepted. The request for the meaning of a religious belief is logically prior to the question of accepting that belief on faith or to the question of whether that belief constitutes knowledge. This point the philosophical analysts have driven home with a vengeance.

Contemporary religious and Christian scholars have recognized that the concern of analytic philosophers with language and meaning is (in the words of Professor Dirks, Editor of *The Christian Scholar*) not "merely the fragile and controversial furnishings for a side-show of the community of scholars." [1] On the contrary, the issues raised and discussed by the analysts are of fundamental import for the religious believer, Christian or other. These issues are not merely academic; they have profound implications for the religious life. They expose "some of the deepest perplexities of thoughtful persons in the age in which we live." Although the ordinary practicing religious believer is not in any degree troubled by the perplexities of religious language (among the reasons for this, I would suggest, are that he is uninformed on the issues involved, or that he operates implicitly or explicitly within the framework of anthropomorphism), the religious scholars are very much troubled. With their more sophisticated conception of religion, they are puzzled about whether religious concepts have objective import, about the meaning-status of religious statements, and about the sense in which they can be said to be true. The Christian scholar in particular wants to know "whether Christian faith is the result of talking oneself out of anxiety by the entertainment of unreal supposition, or whether something that is true is claimed and can be meaningfully supported as true in the thought, worship, and practice of a Christian." [2]

The activities of analytic philosophers are not necessarily antithetical to religion and theology. To be sure, the positivist's brand of analysis resulted in a wholesale dismissal of religious and theological claims as nonsense. However, the more recent brand of analysis—in which meaning is identified with use—not only does not arbitrarily reject religion but also may be in some sense quite compatible with religion. Emphasizing that "each statement has its own logic," and avoiding the categorizing of all statements into a few cupboards, contemporary analysts attempt to meet religion on its own grounds. There is no necessary connection between analytic philosophy and religious skepticism. This is not to say, however, that an analysis of what religious believers and theologians

[1] J. Edward Dirks, "The Relevance of Contemporary Analytic Philosophy for the Community of Christian Scholars," *The Christian Scholar,* vol. 43 (1960), p. 164.

[2] *Ibid.*

say—i.e., the uses of religious concepts and statements—will unquestionably support the cognitive status of religious beliefs, but only that such an analysis gives religion a fairer hearing.

In this book we will be concerned with the impact of philosophical analysis upon religion, analysis as it is found in the tradition of logical positivism and analysis as it is found in the writings of the later Wittgenstein and his followers. We will characterize the principal tenets of positivism, the development and changes in the doctrine, and the current form in which it has survived, especially as it is affecting religion (chapters Two and Seven). We will characterize conceptual analysis as it is found in the writings of Wittgenstein, Ryle, Wisdom, and others (chapter Three), examining the analyses of religious discourse of a number of contemporary philosophers who accept this method of analysis (chapter Six). In all this our purpose will be that of posing and attempting to answer the traditional philosophical question of whether there is religious knowledge. Our program for doing this will involve four basic steps. First, we will attempt to define religious beliefs, differentiating them from beliefs of other kinds and classifying them according to type (chapter Four). Second, we will ask whether religious beliefs have cognitive or factual significance. This will involve a discussion of the problem of cognitivity, devising and justifying a test or set of criteria for cognitive or factual significance, and then ascertaining whether religious beliefs conform to that test or set of criteria (chapter Five). Third, we will discuss the problem of epistemology, the issue of acceptable criteria for the application of the term "knowledge" to beliefs, and the vindication of those criteria (chapter Eight). Fourth, we will ask whether religious beliefs conform to the criteria for knowledge (chapter Eight). Answering those questions is tantamount to answering the question of whether there is religious knowledge.

CHAPTER TWO

Logical Positivism and Religion

The movement known as logical positivism has had a long and interesting history. It developed out of the discussion of the "Vienna Circle," led by Moritz Schlick, Professor of Philosophy at Vienna. Since the 1920's the movement has undergone many and varied changes, and it is in fact questionable that a single contemporary philosopher can be called a positivist in the old sense of the phrase. Even the charter members of the circle (Carnap and Feigl) have altered their views almost beyond recognition. The movement, however, has had tremendous impact in various areas of philosophy (ethics, philosophy of science, aesthetics, philosophy of religion, epistemology, and metaphysics) and its influence is still being felt even in the mild form in which it exists today. This is especially true in the area of religion; philosophers of religion and theologians are still smarting under the request that religious claims be shown to have empirical content or factual meaning. In this chapter we will attempt to characterize the essential elements of the positivistic movement, the key changes which the movement has undergone, and the impact it has had upon theology and religious discourse.

As Bergmann indicates, the label "logical positivist" is applied to philosophers who represent a wide range of interests and who often disagree on the right answer or about the proper method to employ to arrive at it.[1] It is not, then, without some danger of misrepre-

[1] Gustav Bergmann, "Logical Positivism," in his *The Metaphysics of Logical Positivism* (New York: Longmans, Green & Co., Inc., 1954), p. 1; reprinted from V. Ferm, ed., *A History of Philosophical Systems,* (New York: Philosophical Library, Inc., 1950), pp. 471-82.

sentation that we undertake our task. There are, however, certain fundamental beliefs which are held by those philosophers called positivists, and these we will attempt to make clear.

Two of the principal aspects of logical positivism are its conception of philosophy as "logical analysis"—the clarification of Language—and the rejection of metaphysics as meaningless. These two aspects are closely tied together, for the positivist's conception of logical analysis leads him to the conclusion that metaphysical claims are meaningless. What is meant by logical analysis? Carnap remarks that "the function of logical analysis is to analyze all knowledge, all assertions of science and of everyday life, in order to make clear the sense of each such assertion and the connection between them." [2] Schlick remarks that "science should be defined as 'the pursuit of truth' and philosophy as 'the pursuit of meaning.' " [3] Wittgenstein, in his *Tractatus,* tells us that "Philosophy does not result in 'philosophical propositions' but rather in the clarification of propositions." [4] What, however, does it mean to "make propositions clear" or "pursue meaning"? The positivist's answer is admittedly tied to Hume's empiricism and his distinction between matters of fact and relations of ideas. Hume stated that when he "suspects that any philosophical term has no idea annexed to it (as is too common) he always asks *from what impression that idea is derived? And if no impression* can be produced, he concludes that the term is altogether insignificant. 'Tis after this method he examines our idea of *substance* and *essence,* and it were to be wished that this rigorous method were more practical in all philosophical debates." [5] This "rigorous method" of Hume is encompassed in the empirical verifiability criterion of meaning. Its early formulation by Schlick is, "The meaning of a Proposition is the method of its Verification." [6]

[2] Rudolf Carnap, *Philosophy and Logical Syntax* (London: Routledge & Kegan Paul, Ltd., 1935), p. 9.

[3] Moritz Schlick, "The Future of Philosophy," in *Gesammelte Aufsatze* (Vienna, 1938), p. 126.

[4] Ludwig Wittgenstein, *Tractatus Logico-Philosophicus,* a new translation by D. F. Pears and B. F. McGuiness (London: Routledge & Kegan Paul, 1961), 4, 112. Originally published in German in the final number of Ostwald's *Annalen Der Naturphilosophie,* 1921. Hereafter cited as *Tractatus.*

[5] David Hume, *An Abstract of a Treatise of Human Nature,* ed. J. M. Keynes and P. Sraffa (London: Macmillan & Co., Ltd., 1938), p. 11.

[6] Schlick, *op. cit.,* p. 181.

"We know the meaning of a proposition," he goes on to say, "when we are able to indicate exactly the circumstances under which it would be true (or what amounts to the same thing the circumstances under which it would be false). The description of these circumstances is absolutely the only way in which the meaning of a sentence can be made clear." [7] Wittgenstein stated almost the same thing in the *Tractatus* in these words: "To understand a proposition means to know what is the case if it is true." [8] Waismann drew the obvious conclusion that "if there is no possible way to determine whether a statement is true then that statement has no meaning whatsoever." [9] Schlick made the position crystal clear: "A genuine statement must be capable of conclusive verification." [10]

It was quickly seen that this verification test had insuperable difficulties confronting it. To be sure, it ruled out as meaningless all metaphysical statements. But what of "universal" laws, scientific laws, or any sentences of universal form? They also had to be characterized as meaningless because they are incapable of conclusive verification. Schlick drew exactly this inference. Laws or sentences of a universal form are merely instructions for forming statements.[11] They are not themselves factually meaningful statements. Universal laws were viewed as "important nonsense." Carnap and others refused to accept this view of hypotheses or laws of nature and, in his "Testability and Meaning," we find Carnap substituting the word "confirmation" for "verification." [12] Reichenbach helped this substitution along by pointing out that practically the entire body of scientific assertions must be considered meaningless under the verifiability principle.[13] "Confirmability," substituted for "conclusive verification," avoided these self-stultifying consequences. In fact, the confirmability requirement did not insist upon either

[7] *Ibid.*, p. 127.

[8] *Tractatus*, 4.024.

[9] F. Waismann, in *Erkenntnis*, vol. 1 (1930), p. 229, quoted by Karl Popper, in his *The Logic of Scientific Discovery* (New York: Basic Books, Inc., 1959), p. 40; originally published in German in 1931 as *Logik der Forschung*.

[10] M. Schlick, in *Naturwissenschaften*, vol. 19 (1931), p. 150, quoted by Popper, *op. cit.*

[11] Schlick, *Ibid.*, quoted by Popper, *op. cit.*, p. 37.

[12] *Philosophy of Science*, Vol. 3 (1936) and Vol. 4 (1937).

[13] *Philosophy of Science*, Vol. 3 (1936), p. 125.

complete verification or actual confirmation (incomplete verification), but simply upon possible (logically possible) verification. Popper's thesis of "falsifiability" is very close to Carnap's confirmability test.[14] The demand that there must be a way of falsifying a proposition is similar to the demand that there must be a way of confirming it, for the proposition which (if true) confirms another proposition will (if false) falsify it. The claim that we can falsify hypotheses, not prove them, is reasonably close to saying that hypotheses can be confirmed, not proven or conclusively verified.[15]

A similar modification of the verification thesis was set forth by Ayer in his *Language, Truth and Logic*.[16] Ayer distinguished between a "weak" and "strong" sense of verifiable, insisting that the verification principle embody only the "weak" sense. The "strong" sense amounted to conclusive verification; the "weak" sense insisted only that some empirical observation be relevant to a given claim, or that one could say what it would be like to verify it. Ayer in fact later recognized that the distinction between the "weak" and "strong" sense of verifiable wasn't a genuine distinction. The "strong" sense is logically impossible, because an empirical proposition (with the exception of "protocol" statements—statements which describe nothing other than one's immediate experience) is defined as one which is always subject to the test of further experiences.

Ayer, along with Reichenbach, introduced other qualifications and clarifications of the verifiability principle. Ayer distinguished between practical verifiability and verifiability in principle;[17] Reichenbach between three sorts of impossibilities in verification—technical, physical, and logical.[18] Both agree that there are many propositions which, for technical, physical, or practical reasons, cannot be verified but which are perfectly meaningful. Ayer cites as an example the proposition that there are mountains on the other

[14] Popper, *op. cit.*

[15] John Passmore, "Logical Positivism (1)," *The Australasian Journal of Psychology and Philosophy*, Vol. 21 (1943), p. 87.

[16] A. J. Ayer, *Language, Truth and Logic*, second edition (London: Victor Gollancz, Ltd., 1946), pp. 9 and 37.

[17] *Ibid.*, p. 36.

[18] H. Reichenbach, *Experience and Prediction: An Analysis of the Foundations and the Structure of Knowledge* (Chicago: University of Chicago Press, 1938).

side of the moon. We do not have the physical or practical means to make the relevant observations to verify this proposition. But we do know what observations would verify or falsify the proposition; that is, the proposition is verifiable in principle. It is logically possible to verify it. There are other propositions, however, which logically preclude any possible verification. They are not verifiable in principle. Ayer cites from F. H. Bradley this example: "The Absolute enters into, but is itself incapable of, evolution and progress."[19] One cannot even conceive of (much less *have*) an observation which would enable one to determine whether the Absolute did or did not enter into evolution or progress. Such an experience is logically precluded. Statements of this sort can have no literal factual meaning. They may, very well, however, have *emotive meaning,* or express the way one feels.

The verification principle, however, even in its modified form, excluded the meaningfulness of mathematics, geometry, and logic; for none of the propositions in these areas is verified by references to any possible experience. The positivists, therefore, made a distinction between empirically verifiable propositions and "analytic" or a priori propositions. The latter are "true by definition" or true by virtue of a set of axioms, postulates, or premises. "All equiangular triangles are equilateral" is an example of an analytic truth. One does not verify this proposition by observation. It is true by virtue of the framework of Euclidean geometry. Ayer, then, reformulates the meaning criterion so that a sentence has literal meaning if and only if the proposition it expresses is either analytic or empirically verifiable.[20] Feigl turns the same trick by distinguishing between two kinds of "cognitive meaning"—formal, logico-arithmetical meaning, and factual or empirical meaning. He insists, in fact, that "many an epistemological question has been obscured by mistaking logico-mathematical for factual meaning."[21] The distinction between these two kinds of cognitive meaning, and a recognition of the noncognitive function or meaning of much language, will clear

[19] Ayer, *op. cit.,* p. 36.

[20] *Ibid.,* p. 9.

[21] H. Feigl, "Logical Empiricism," in *Twentieth Century Philosophy,* edited by D. D. Runes (New York: Philosophical Library, Inc., 1943), p. 379.

up confusion and "erroneous pretense." "Many metaphysical 'problems' and their 'solutions' depend upon the erroneous presumption of the presence of factual meaning in expressions which have only emotive appeals and/or a formally correct grammatical structure." [22] The philosopher must be on the lookout for sentences which generate this confusion—sentences which actually violate the syntactical rules of a given language, sentences which are grammatically or syntactically correct but which are not verifiable in principle, and sentences which appear to have factual meaning but which really have emotive meaning only. Armed with this account of the meaning of "meaning," the positivists proceeded to eliminate metaphysics.

The Elimination of Metaphysics

The conclusion of the positivist that he has eliminated metaphysics follows logically from his account of meaning and his analysis of metaphysical claims as being neither analytic nor empirically verifiable. For the most part, the positivists identified metaphysics with a kind of transcendentalism, the view that reality is something other than the sensory world and that the metaphysician-philosopher can provide us with knowledge of this transcendent world. The positivist's reply to the metaphysician is simply that "no statement which refers to a reality transcending the limits of all possible sense experience can possibly have any literal significance, from which it follows that the labours of those who have striven to describe such a reality have all been devoted to the production of nonsense." [23] Metaphysics is eliminated as nonsense simply by formulating "the criterion which enables us to test whether a sentence expresses a genuine proposition about a matter of fact, and then pointing out that the sentences under consideration fail to satisfy it." [24]

The philosopher, the positivist claims, is not a scientist. He does not provide us with knowledge of the universe. Those thinkers who

[22] *Ibid.*
[23] Ayer, *op. cit.*, p. 34.
[24] *Ibid.*, p. 35

identify philosophy with a kind of super-science—who maintain that "philosophy differs from the sciences nowise in its spirit but only in its boundaries, in dealing with certain comprehensive features of experience which lie outside the purview of the special sciences" [25]—are the ones who generate confusion and nonsense. *Real* philosophy dispels this nonsense and introduces clarity. As Wittgenstein puts it, "The correct method of philosophy would really be the following: to say nothing except what can be said, i.e., propositions of natural science—i.e., something that has nothing to do with philosophy—and then, whenever someone else wanted to say something metaphysical, to demonstrate to him that he had failed to give a meaning to certain signs in his propositions." [26] The principal tool for such demonstration is the empirical verifiability criterion of meaning. It is not the only tool. Philosophical confusion can also be dispelled by an analysis of the structure of our language. Wittgenstein in fact claims that "Most of the propositions and questions of philosophers arise from our failure to understand the logic of our language." [27] Ayer similarly claims that philosophical pseudo-problems result from taking "the grammatical structure of the sentence as a trustworthy guide to . . . meaning." [28] We must get beneath the "surface grammar" and understand the "logic of our language." Then many philosophical issues traditionally discussed are seen as "fictitious" problems. Take, for example, the long-standing realist-idealist controversy. This controversy can be seen to be fictitious on two grounds. First, in the words of Carnap, "while from the assertion of the reality or the existence of kangaroos we can *deduce* perceptive propositions, from the assertion of the Reality of the physical world this is not possible; neither is it possible from the opposite assertion of the Unreality of the physical world. Therefore both assertions have no empirical content—no sense at all." [29] Secondly, to paraphrase Ayer, simply because it so

[25] S. Alexander, *Space, Time and Deity*, Introduction, p. 4; quoted by John Passmore, "Logical Positivism (11)," in *The Australasian Journal of Psychology and Philosophy*, Vol. 22 (1944), p. 129.

[26] *Tractatus*, 6.53.

[27] *Tractatus*, 4.003.

[28] Ayer, *op. cit.*, p. 51.

[29] R. Carnap, *op. cit.*, p. 20.

happens that in our English language we describe things by using the grammatical form of subject and predicate, we assume that it is necessary to make a distinction between the thing itself (thus the metaphysical notion of "substance") and its sensible properties.[30] Actually, Ayer claims, the so-called problem of substance and the realist-idealist controversy can really be reduced to "a dispute concerning the analysis of existential propositions, and so a logical problem which can be definitely solved. . . ." [31]

One method suggested by Ayer for solving such "logical problems" is that of formulating "definitions in use." He states:

> We define a symbol in use not by saying that it is synonymous with some other symbol, but by showing that the sentences in which it significantly occurs can be translated into equivalent sentences, which contain neither the definiendum itself, nor any of its synonyms.[32]

Such definitions in use "dispel those confusions which arise from our imperfect understanding of certain types of sentences in our language . . ." [33] Ayer cites Russell's theory of descriptions as an example of this method. Russell translates sentences of the form "the so and so" into a definition in use so that they are no longer ambiguous. Thus "the round-square cannot exist" is translated into the equivalent (but clarified form) "no one thing can be both round and square." The pseudo-problem of the existence or subsistence of round-square is avoided by the translation. Some philosophers, who assume that the round-square must at least subsist if we are to speak of it, lapse into metaphysics (theory of universals) in the naïve assumption that definite descriptive phrases are demonstrative symbols or names. The technique of definitions in use gets us beneath the "surface grammar" of language, reveals its logical complexities, and prevents our being led into these mistaken assumptions about the world. The whole bag of philosophical or metaphysical problems, including the question of the reality of universals, the reality of numbers, the reality of other minds, the subjective-objec-

[30] Ayer, *op. cit.*, p. 42.
[31] *Ibid.*, p. 40.
[32] *Ibid.*, p. 60.
[33] *Ibid.*, p. 62.

tive controversy in ethics, and the rationalist-empiricist controversy, can be resolved by the analysis and clarification of language. Such analysis involves the application of the empirical verifiability criterion of meaning, the application of the definition-in-use technique, and other methods (Ayer cites, for example, G. E. Moore's analysis of "exists" as an appropriate technique, although admittedly "nothing even approaching a definition is either provided or sought").[34] The result of the positivist's philosophical analysis is the elimination of metaphysics. The only exception is "inductive metaphysics," and this species of metaphysics is characterized as "merely the risky, sanguine, disreputable extreme of science."[35]

The Elimination of Theology

For the positivist it follows analytically that if metaphysical claims are eliminated as "bad grammar" or as cognitively meaningless, theological claims are likewise eliminated; for theology is but one species of metaphysics. Religious or theological statements, in order to have cognitive meaning, must be either analytic or a priori (in which case they are tautologically true), or empirical propositions (in which case it must be shown that such claims are verifiable in principle). The religious do not set forth their claims as tautologies. Such claims cannot be empirical, for they are purportedly about a transcendent being, a being who is "beyond" the empirical world. As Ayer puts it, ". . . the term 'god' is a metaphysical term. And if 'god' is a metaphysical term, then it cannot be even probable that a god exists. For to say that 'God exists' is to make a metaphysical utterance which cannot be either true or false."[36] The positivist then draws the inference that religious claims about God have no cognitive meaning whatever. They have emotive meaning only.

Ayer insists that the positivistic view of religious assertions—that all statements about the nature of God are nonsensical—not be confused with the view of the atheist or of the agnostic. "For it is

[34] *Ibid.*, p. 24.
[35] Feigl, *op. cit.*, p. 729.
[36] Ayer, *op. cit.*, p. 115.

characteristic of an agnostic to hold that the existence of a God is a possibility in which there is no good reason either to believe or disbelieve; and it is characteristic of an atheist to hold that it is at least probable that no god exists."[37] The positivist's position is incompatible with both agnosticism and atheism, for while the former maintains that religious statements are nonsensical, the latter two maintain that such statements are meaningful (empirically meaningful) but either probably false (atheism) or such that we cannot say, on the basis of our present evidence, whether they are true or false (agnosticism). Ayer does not offer the religious the comfort offered by either the agnostic or atheist. The only "comfort" that can be offered is that: since the theologian "says nothing at all about the world, he cannot justly be accused of saying anything false, or anything for which he has insufficient grounds."[38] This is really a way of saying that the positivistic critique undercuts religion at a much more fundamental point than either atheism or agnosticism.

On occasion theologians do relate their religious claims to actual or possible experiences. The positivist admits this, and agrees that in these cases in which God or the religious object is identified with natural or observable phenomena, the religious assertion is cognitively significant. Ayer gives this example: "If . . . a man tells me that the occurrence of thunder is alone both necessary and sufficient to establish the truth of the proposition that Jehovah is angry, I may conclude that, in his usage of the words, the sentence 'Jehovah is angry' is equivalent to 'It is thundering.' "[39] So interpreted, this claim has empirical meaning. But the fact is that in "sophisticated religions" God is not identified with natural phenomena. He controls the world but is himself transcendent, and thus the assertion of his existence or of his attributes cannot be reduced to the assertion of regularity in nature or the occurrence of natural phenomena. If, however, religious claims cannot be so reduced in meaning, then they are, of necessity, senseless, for ". . . the notion of a person

[37] *Ibid.*
[38] *Ibid.*, p. 118.
[39] *Ibid.*

whose essential attributes are nonempirical is not an intelligible notion at all."[40]

Ayer, I think, is correct in his claim that what the theist wants to assert goes beyond the assertion of the occurrence of natural or observable phenomena. What is this "something else"? One reply by the religious is that the factual content of religious claims is known through mystical experience or religious visions. God is known in mystical intuition and cannot be characterized in human terms. The positivist's response here is twofold. First, he agrees that an empirical truth may be discovered by purely intuitive methods as well as by the method of induction. Secondly, however, he insists that by whatever means a proposition is arrived at, it must be empirically testable. Thus Ayer states: "We do not deny *a priori* that the mystic is able to discover truths by his own special methods. We wait to hear what are the propositions which embody his discoveries, in order to see whether they are verified or confuted by our empirical observation. But the mystic, so far from producing propositions which are empirically verified, is unable to produce any intelligible propositions at all."[41] The mystic and those philosophers who "fill their books" with assertions which they know intuitively merely provide material for the psychoanalyst.[42]

The Status of the Verifiability Principle

A number of philosophers and theologians have been sharply critical of the positivist's analysis of metaphysics and theology. It has been noted that the positivist's conclusion that metaphysical and theological statements are cognitively meaningless follows analytically from the acceptance of the empirical verifiability criterion as an adequate account of meaning. As Professor Lazerowitz remarks:

> His (Ayer's) demonstration turns out to be both an explanation of and justification for a new use of "nonsense" which, because it is

[40] *Ibid.*
[41] *Ibid.*
[42] *Ibid.*, p. 118.

> stated in the form of a demonstration, effectively conceals what is being done, from himself as well as from others. His "conclusion," then, turns out to be a linguistic innovation: it introduces us to the positivistic use of "nonsense," according to which "nonsensical indicative sentence" means the same as "indicative sentence which expresses neither an *a priori* nor an empirical proposition." [43]

Ayer himself, in his second edition of *Language, Truth and Logic,* recognizes the tautological nature of his critique of metaphysics and theology when he points out that, if another criterion of meaning is adopted, and "if a statement satisfied such a criterion, there is, no doubt, some proper use of the word 'understanding' in which it would be capable of being understood." [44] This is equivalent to saying that his conclusion that metaphysics is nonsense might not follow from a different criterion of meaning. The crucial issue is that of the acceptability of the positivist's account of meaning. Philosophers and theologians, therefore, have been led to ask, "What is the logical status of the verification principle itself?" Why should the principle be accepted? Many have been concerned over the blanket indictment of all theology and all metaphysics, an indictment not substantiated by a careful study of what theologians and metaphysicians have said. Crombie, for example, refers to Ayer as the wolf "who would devour as meaningless all theological statements in one meal," [45] and Passmore points out that the only metaphysician Carnap criticizes in detail is Heidegger, and furthermore that Thales, Bradley, and other metaphysicians will not agree that they have cut all connection between their beliefs or statements and experience.[46] The positivists themselves, in their later writings, agree that a fairer treatment of theologians and metaphysicians requires a close and careful scrutiny of the statements of each, even the attempt to translate what the metaphysician says into clearer

[43] M. Lazerowitz, "The Positivist Use of Nonsense," in *Mind,* Vol. 55 (1946), p. 254.

[44] Ayer, *op. cit.,* p. 16.

[45] I. M. Crombie, "The Possibility of Theological Statements," in *Faith and Logic,* edited by Basil Mitchell (London: George Allen & Unwin, Ltd., 1957), p. 77.

[46] John Passmore, "Logical Positivism (11)," in *op. cit.,* pp. 141-142.

language. Too quick a cry of "nonsense" is a hindrance, not a help, in the development of empirical theory.[47]

What of the status of the verification principle itself? Some critics applied the principle to itself, asking whether it itself is an analytic or empirical statement. The positivists explicitly denied that the principle was to be considered as an empirical hypothesis.[48] Nor were they happy to treat it as an analytic truth. The principle is not an *assertion* of any kind. Some critics drew the obvious inference that the empirical verifiability criterion was itself cognitively meaningless, or that it has emotive meaning only. Ayer himself wants the principle accepted as a definition, not as an entirely arbitrary one at that. In the second edition of *Language, Truth and Logic,* he explicitly leaves open the possibility, even the fact, that there are other senses of "meaning" in common use and that "it is open to anyone to adopt a different criterion of meaning and so produce an alternative definition which may very well correspond to one of the ways in which the word meaning is commonly used." [49] However, only if statements satisfy the verification principle are they "capable of being understood in the sense in which either scientific hypotheses or common-sense statements are habitually understood." [50] The suggestion is that if one is interested in scientific hypotheses or common-sense statements, then it would be fruitful to adopt the verifiability thesis. Stevenson puts his finger exactly on the issue in these words:

> Shall we define "meaning" narrowly, so that science alone will receive this laudatory title, and metaphysics the corresponding derogatory one of "nonsense." Shall our terminology show science in a fine light and metaphysics in a poor one? Shall we, in short, accept this persuasive definition of meaning? [51]

Stevenson's reply to this question is that the positivist's thesis will shed "not only heat but light" if it is used as a way of drawing our

[47] *Ibid.*, p. 149.
[48] Ayer, *op. cit.*, p. 16.
[49] *Ibid.*
[50] *Ibid.*
[51] Charles Stevenson, "Persuasive Definitions," in *Mind,* Vol. 47 (1938), p. 339.

attention "to the fundamental differences between the use of sen tences in science and their use in metaphysics." This can be done without employing the "objectionable emotive meaning" of the word "nonsense" as applied to metaphysics, and by carefully examining both the nature of science and the nature of metaphysics.

The positivist's position has also been criticized on the grounds that, although it purports to eliminate metaphysics, it is itself a disguised metaphysic. To be sure, the positivist claims that all that he is doing is logical analysis, the clarification of language. The propositions which the positivist considers to need analysis are, as Passmore notes,

> those which lead to inferences which are false, to questions which are spurious, to assumptions which are nonsensical. And it follows that the analyst must begin by deciding which inferences *are* false, which questions *are* spurious, which assumptions *are* nonsensical: to particularize, he must argue against the validity of ontological arguments, must show that there are no "subsistent entities," that it is "nonsense" to talk of a physical world. In other words, the problems which confront him are precisely those which traditional philosophy has tried to answer; and until he finds some answer to them, the analyst does not know how to clarify our language.[52]

The positivist, Passmore is suggesting, is not merely an analyst or clarifier. He fails "to provide a clear line of demarcation between philosophy as 'the pursuit of meaning' and science as 'the pursuit of truth'—because to pursue meanings is to pursue truth"; nor does he avoid the traditional problems of philosophy.[53] He himself invokes a metaphysical position, the metaphysic of logical atomism,[54] which he uses as a point of reference for his "analysis."

More recently the verifiability criterion has been so modified that it can no longer be viewed as a stick with which to beat the metaphysician. Feigl suggests that a proposition is meaningful if it implies observable consequences; it itself need not assert something

[52] John Passmore, "Logical Positivism (II)," in *op. cit.*, p. 136.

[53] *Ibid.*

[54] See John Wisdom, "Metaphysics and Verification," in *Mind*, Vol. 47 (1938); G. Bergmann, *op. cit.;* and J. O. Urmson, *Philosophical Analysis, Its Development Between the Two World Wars* (New York: Oxford University Press, 1956).

observable. The scientist must use hypothetical constructs, and such constructs are anchored in only a few places in observation. "The cognitive content of theories cannot be translated into observation statements." [55] What wider door does the metaphysician need? Hempel, along the same lines, states that "most scientific hypotheses do not even by implication assert any observation sentence at all," and suggests that

> . . . cognitive significance in the sense intended by recent empiricism and operationism can best be attributed to sentences forming a theoretical system, and perhaps rather to such systems as wholes. . . . We will further have to recognize that cognitive significance in a system is a matter of degree: Significant systems range from those whose entire extra-logical vocabulary consists of observation terms, through theories whose formulation relies heavily on theoretical constructs, on to systems with hardly any bearing on potential empirical findings.[56]

For Hempel cognitive significance is best applied to systems and is a matter of degree. The least arbitrary and most fruitful way of appraising different systems is by reference to these characteristics: (a) "the clarity and precision with which the theories are formulated . . ."; (b) "the systematic, i.e., explanatory and predictive, power of the systems in regard to observable phenomena"; (c) "the formal simplicity of the theoretical system"; and (d) "the extent to which the theories have been confirmed by experimental evidence." [57] It is Hempel's contention that much of traditional metaphysics and "speculative philosophical approaches to cosmology, biology, or history . . . would make a poor showing on practically all these counts. . . ." [58]

Note, however, that Hempel does not dogmatically reject metaphysics or "speculative philosophical approaches." Even metaphysical and theological theories or systems would have *some degree* of

[55] H. Feigl, "Philosophical Embarrassments of Psychology," *American Psychologist,* vol. 14, no. 3 (1959), p. 127.

[56] Carl G. Hempel, "The Concept of Cognitive Significance," *Proceedings of the American Academy of Arts and Sciences,* Vol. 80 (1951), p. 74. Reprinted by permission.

[57] *Ibid.*

[58] *Ibid.*

cognitive significance, although they would not conform to the proposed criteria *as well* as most scientific theories. Hempel's reformulated positivism has the effect of stressing the differences between various uses of language—scientific, metaphysical, political, etc.—without arbitrarily rejecting any particular use. To paraphrase Stevenson, Hempel's approach sheds more light than heat. It leads to the recognition of the rich variety of the uses of language—to that extent jibing with the later Wittgenstein and Oxford view that meaning is use—and avoids the attempt of trying to fit all statements into a few categories.

Logical positivism, then, has come a long way since the 1920's. No longer do the philosophers in this tradition *arbitrarily* reject metaphysics, theology, and religion. They are still concerned with whether metaphysical and theological statements have cognitive significance. Many still claim that such statements have no predictive value and are in fact compatible with any state of affairs, and hence are devoid of factual meaning. That form of positivism which is at present challenging religion and theology is found in the falsifiability challenge. We noted that Popper first formulated the principle of falsifiability. The contemporary critic of religion applies this principle by asking of the religious what occurrences would tend to falsify or be incompatible with their claims. This challenge is well illustrated in Antony Flew's paraphrase of a parable originally told by Professor Wisdom:

> Once upon a time two explorers came upon a clearing in the jungle. In the clearing were growing many flowers and many weeds. One explorer says, "Some gardener must tend this plot." The other disagrees, "There is no gardener." So they pitch their tents and set a watch. No gardener is ever seen. "But perhaps he is an invisible gardener." So they set up a barbed-wire fence. They patrol it with bloodhounds. (For they remember how H. G. Wells' *The Invisible Man* could be both smelt and touched though he could not be seen.) But no shrieks ever suggest that some intruder has received a shock. No movements of the wire ever betray an invisible climber. The bloodhounds never give cry. Yet still the Believer is not convinced. "But there is a gardener, invisible, intangible, insensible to electric shocks, a gardener who has no scent and makes no sound, a gardener who comes secretly to look after the garden which he loves." At last the Sceptic despairs, "But what

> remains of your original assertion? Just how does what you call an invisible, intangible, eternally elusive gardener differ from an imaginary gardener or even from no gardener at all?"[59]

Responses to this challenge (by those both within and outside the faith), a challenge which requires that the religious at least be able to point to data which are incompatible with the claim that God exists or the claim that God has certain attributes, have been varied and extremely interesting. We will examine these responses in detail in chapters seven and eight.

[59] A. Flew, "Theology and Falsification," in *New Essays in Philosophical Theology,* edited by A. Flew and A. MacIntyre (New York: The Macmillan Company, 1955), p. 96.

CHAPTER THREE

Conceptual Analysis and Religion

It is an acknowledged fact that the greatest single influence on contemporary Anglo-Saxon philosophy is that of Ludwig Wittgenstein. This influence is in large part a result of his later work, *Philosophische Untersuchungen* or *Philosophical Investigations.*[1] His earlier work, *Tractatus Logicus Philosophicus,* represents a position which he later came to reject almost in toto. In the *Tractatus* Wittgenstein, under the influence of Bertrand Russell, attempted to formulate a logically perfect language. Our ordinary language, which contains vague and ambiguous symbols and which permits nonsensical combinations of symbols, is inaccurate. The philosopher's function is that of constructing an ideal language in which ambiguity and inaccuracy are precluded.

This ideal language was part of the total philosophical position known as "logical atomism," adopted by both Wittgenstein and Russell. Essential to this position is what is generally characterized as "the picture theory of meaning." There is, Wittgenstein tells us, a kind of correspondence between the elements in a picture and the elements of the object or scene it depicts. Furthermore, the picture reflects the arrangement or the structure of the objects in the world. Now, "A state of affairs (a state of things) is a combination of objects (things). . . . The configuration of objects produces states of affairs [atomic facts]." [2] Corresponding to the atomic facts in the

[1] Ludwig Wittgenstein, *Philosophical Investigations,* published posthumously (Oxford: Basil Blackwell & Mott, Ltd., 1953), with German and English texts facing. English translation by G. E. M. Anscombe.

[2] *Tractatus,* 2.01; 2.0272.

world are atomic propositions which picture those facts. Atomic, or elementary, propositions are composed of names connected or structured in a certain manner. In order to be accurate, the structure of the proposition must picture the structure of atomic facts or states of affairs in the world. The propositions of any language are either atomic propositions which picture atomic facts, or truth-functional compounds of atomic propositions. All meaningful discourse is derivable in the last analysis from atomic propositions and the naming relation. Language not so reducible has no meaning. (At this stage Wittgenstein is really a positivist, for as Urmson points out, "The verification principle can be stated as a consequence of the atomic hypothesis in metaphysics. . . ." [3]) In formulating this ideal language, Wittgenstein insists, the concern of the philosopher is not with the truth or falsity of statements about the world. This is the concern of the scientist. The philosopher's concern is simply analysis, clarification, and the specification of that which is necessary for meaningful discourse.

In the *Philosophical Investigations,* Wittgenstein came to reject the view that the task of the philosopher is to correct or reform ordinary language. In fact, even in the *Tractatus* there is ambivalence in his thought, for on one occasion he states that "all propositions of our everyday language, just as they stand, are in perfect logical order." [4] In the *Philosophical Investigations,* however, he clearly rejects the view that ordinary language needs reforming into an ideal language. He states, in fact, that there are "grave mistakes" in the *Tractatus,* and included among those mistakes is the entire picture theory of meaning, the atomistic view of language in which the concept of "naming" is central, and the view that a language must have the clear structure of a logical calculus. Language has more than one function than that of picturing or naming. It has many functions or uses, and it is the task of the philosopher to portray these multiple functions or uses. Philosophical problems, in fact, are generated by inattention to and consequent misuse of language. Wittgenstein invites us to replace the notion of meaning with the notion of use. "For a large class of cases—though not for all—

[3] J. O. Urmson, *Philosophical Analysis,* IV, 54, p. 109.
[4] *Tractatus,* 5.5563.

in which we employ the term 'meaning' it can be defined thus: the meaning of a word is its use in the language." [5] Once this replacement is effected, we become able to understand and to avoid the sources of philosophical confusions, for such confusions arise as a result of ignoring the use, context, or "language-game" which give our words significance. Not recognizing that the meaning of an expression is its use in some actual language-game, we might become puzzled (and the philosopher does) as to how certain apparently obvious statements (like "I know he is in great pain") can be intelligible. Wittgenstein simply reminds us that in our ordinary language-games we do know how to use such words, and their significance poses no problem. Philosophers become puzzled because they remove our language from the ordinary context and use which give it its meaning, thus involving themselves in conceptual tangles. When such misuse occurs, Wittgenstein asks, "But what are these words to be used for now? The language-game in which they are to be applied is missing." [6] These conceptual tangles also result from being misled by what Wittgenstein calls the "surface grammar" of expressions, which causes one to overlook the immensely complex and numerous uses that language has, and even to attempt to reduce all uses of language to one model (which Wittgenstein himself attempted in the *Tractatus*). When philosophers become puzzled about certain concepts or statements (concepts like "good," "real," "solid," and "true"), Wittgenstein advises them to ask themselves, "How did we learn the meaning of this word ('good' for instance)? From what sort of examples; in what language-games?" [7]

For Wittgenstein, philosophical problems result from linguistic or conceptual confusion. Such problems arise "when language goes on a holiday." [8] "The confusions which occupy us arise when language is like an engine idling, not when it is doing its work." [9] Philosophical talk is an idling of the gears of language, a functionless spinning of a wheel disconnected from a mechanism. How are philosophical problems to be solved? Wittgenstein's suggestion is that we re-

[5] *Philosophical Investigations,* p. 20e.
[6] *Ibid.,* p. 44e.
[7] *Ibid.,* p. 36e.
[8] *Ibid.,* p. 19e.
[9] *Ibid.,* p. 51e.

describe the variety of concepts, and their variety of roles or functions. The problematic concepts must be reintroduced into the contexts where they normally function, and their uses and relations with other concepts must be described. Philosophy, for Wittgenstein, becomes a kind of therapy, a way of leading one out of conceptual or linguistic confusions. "Our investigation is therefore a grammatical one. Such an investigation sheds light on our problem by clearing misunderstandings away. Misunderstandings concerning the use of words, caused, among other things, by certain analogies between the forms of expressions in different regions of language." [10] The philosopher need only describe the workings of our language and help us recognize these workings. The problems which have bothered traditional philosophers "are solved, not by giving new information, but by arranging what we have already known. Philosophy is a battle against the bewitchment of our intelligence by means of language." [11]

Wittgenstein himself applied the method of concept analysis to a large number of philosophical problems in his *Philosophical Investigations*. This method of doing philosophy has been (perhaps with some alterations) carried on by Wittgenstein's successor as Professor of Philosophy at Cambridge, John Wisdom. It also has been carried on, again with alterations, by a host of Oxford philosophers, including Gilbert Ryle, John Austin, H. L. A. Hart, P. F. Strawson, S. Hampshire, R. M. Hare, Isiah Berlin, S. E. Toulmin, and P. Nowell-Smith. Concept analysis, or "linguistic analysis" as it is often called, has become the dominant mode of philosophy in Great Britain, and its impact elsewhere, especially in the United States, has been tremendous.

Wisdom accepts Wittgenstein's conception of philosophy as "therapeutic" analysis. In fact, he suggests that philosophical problems or "worries" are to be resolved by a technique similar to the techniques employed by the psychoanalyst in dealing with psychopathic states. The puzzled philosopher, like the neurotic, must be led to recognize the causes of his puzzlement. The philosopher can get out of his state of confused tension by describing "fully the sort of ques-

[10] *Ibid.*, p. 43e.
[11] *Ibid.*, p. 47e.

tion or statement he is considering. By the time he has described this, e.g., has described a philosophical question, he has set it in the language map with regard to all other questions. And then he has answered his own questions. . . . Every philosophical question, when it isn't half asked, answers itself; when it is fully asked, answers itself." [12] Metaphysical difficulties arise when we are confronted with situations in which we do not know what to say—in which our normal language does not seem adequate. What the philosopher must do is describe the situation, pointing to those features which lead us to speak in one way and those which lead us to speak in another way. We must recall the way we use language and why. In fact, philosophical propositions, including the positivist's verification principle, are linguistic proposals. Such proposals (for example, proposals to use the words "know," "true," "good," "meaningful" in certain ways), Wisdom admits, can illuminate our thinking. These proposals should not be viewed as true or false in any absolute sense, as some positivists took them. In fact, to the extent that they are taken as absolute truths or factual truths rather than as linguistic proposals, these philosophical statements are themselves confusions and lead us into perplexities. They should be viewed as useful (or nonuseful) distinctions in illuminating and clarifying experience. Here Wisdom seems to differ somewhat from Wittgenstein. "Wittgenstein," Wisdom tells us, "too much represents them [philosophical confusions] as merely symptoms of linguistic confusion. I wish to represent them as also symptoms of linguistic penetration. . . .[13] The theories of philosophers are illuminating and linguistically penetrating "when they suggest or draw attention to a terminology which reveals likenesses and differences which are concealed by ordinary language."

Of the other philosophers who accept, with modifications, Wittgenstein's conception of philosophy, Oxford's Gilbert Ryle deserves special attention. The affinity between his thought and that of Wittgenstein can be clearly seen in his book, *The Concept of Mind,* in which he attempts to exorcise "the dogma of the Ghost in the Ma-

[12] John Wisdom, *Other Minds* (Oxford: B. H. Blackwell, Ltd., 1952), p. 3, n. 1. See also his *Philosophy and Psycho-Analysis* (Oxford: Basil Blackwell & Mott, Ltd., 1953).

[13] "Philosophical Perplexity," in *Philosophy and Psycho-Analysis,* p. 41.

chine" by analyzing and mapping the concept of mind.[14] But perhaps the affinities and the differences between Ryle and Wittgenstein can best be seen in Ryle's article "Systematically Misleading Expressions." Here he states:

> There are many expressions which occur in non-philosophical discourse which, although they are perfectly clearly understood by those who use them and those who hear or read them, are nevertheless couched in grammatical or syntactical forms which are in a demonstrable way improper to the states of affairs which they record (or the alleged states of affairs which they profess to record). Such expressions can be reformulated, and for philosophy but not for non-philosophical discourse must be reformulated into expressions of which the syntactical form is proper to the facts recorded (or the alleged facts alleged to be recorded).[15]

Take the statement "Carnivorous cows do not exist." This appears to be a statement about a certain kind of thing which is said not to exist, and (in the hands of some philosophers) may lead to the supposition that carnivorous cows must be real in some sense, or it would be unintelligible to say that they do not exist. They must have "subsistent" being. Ryle suggests that the statement "Carnivorous cows do not exist" be reformulated as "Nothing is both a cow and carnivorous." One is not then led into invoking a subsistent realm of existence. The same reformulation must be effected with "quasi-ontological statements" (Mr. Pickwick is a fiction, or Mr. Pickwick is subjective), "quasi-platonic statements" (color involves extension), and other "quasi-descriptions." Grammatically, these kinds of statements may mislead one, for although they have the normal subject-predicate form, this form is really "improper to the states of affairs which they record. . . ."

Note that in this early article Ryle's conception of philosophy involves two functions: (1) clarifying systematically misleading expressions and exposing philosophical absurdities rooted in those expressions, and (2) reformulating language so that it is proper to

[14] G. Ryle, *The Concept of Mind* (London: Hutchinson & Co. Publishers, Ltd., 1949).

[15] Printed in *Logic and Language* (edited by A. G. N. Flew), First Series (Oxford, 1951), p. 14; first published in the *Aristotelian Society Proceedings,* Vol. 32 (1931-32).

the facts. The second, as clearly noted by Urmson, is similar to the doctrine of the logical atomists, the ontological aim of getting a clearer view of the real structure of reality.[16] Ryle later seems to reject the second function. The philosopher does reformulate language which is misleading, but no reference to the form of facts need be involved. That expressions are misleading can be detected without reference to the form of facts. All that one need see is that such expressions, when taken literally, lead one into antinomies and paralogisms.

The basic theory of meaning which Ryle employs in his philosophical analysis is Wittgensteinian—meaning is use. The assumption that all words must mean in the same way as proper names mean (the "Fido-Fido" theory of meaning)[17] is at the source of a great deal of philosophical confusion. Ryle's suggestion, like that of Wittgenstein, is that the philosopher act as therapist by providing a detailed description of the various workings of language, of the various roles which expressions perform. This philosophical therapy, however, cannot be identified with either lexicography or philology. The philosopher is not a compiler of dictionaries, and Ryle is quite concerned that some Oxford philosophers, in what they do, misconstrue the philosopher's interest in "ordinary language." In order to correct this, Ryle, in a recent article, distinguishes between "ordinary use" and "ordinary usage." [18] It is, he claims, a "philosophical howler" to identify the two. The philosopher's interest is not in usage but in use. "The appeal to prevalence is philosophically pointless, besides being philosophically risky. What is wanted is, perhaps, the extraction of the logical rules implicitly governing a concept, i.e., a way of operating with an expression (or any other expression that does the same work). It is probable that the use of this expression is widely current; but whether it is so or not, is of no philosophical interest. Job-analysis is not Mass-Observation." [19] Philosophy is concerned with the "informal logic" of concepts, with "conceptual analysis," or with "logical geographizing." This ac-

[16] J. O. Urmson, *op. cit.*, p. 165.

[17] See G. Ryle, "Theory of Meaning," in *British Philosophy in the Mid-Century*, edited by C. A. Mace (London: George Allen & Unwin, Ltd., 1957).

[18] G. Ryle, "Ordinary Language," in *Philosophical Review*, Vol. 62 (1953).

[19] *Ibid.*, p. 177.

counts, Flew claims, for the fact that philosophy "takes little account of the existence of other languages whose structure and idiom are very different from English . . . but which seem equally if not more capable of engendering metaphysical confusion." [20] In the words of Xenakis, the philosopher deals with linguistic jobs or roles which expressions perform. These roles are "international phenomena," whereas the expressions that do these jobs are not.[21] Thus, when an ordinary language philosopher deals with "true" or "good," he is dealing with the jobs that these concepts perform. When he deals with the role performed by the concept "good," he is at the same time dealing with the role performed by *bon* or *agathon.* In pointing to a "misuse" of a concept, a misuse which generates paradox, perplexity, and confusion, the philosophical analyst is not talking about grammatical misuse but logical misuse. As Flew puts it, "What is complained of is not lack of grammar . . . but incoherence or absence of meaning. . . ." [22]

Ryle and the ordinary language philosopher are not always clear as to how one discovers the "logic" of a concept. The assumption seems to be that all one need do is look—but one must look beyond the "surface grammar" of language. One commentator puts it in this way, "Insufficient attention has been paid to the logical characteristics of these ordinary expressions. *Look* again at these logical characteristics. This is all the appeal to ordinary language amounts to." [23] We do find Wittgenstein, Ryle, and others employing the method of substitution. Wittgenstein states, ". . . substituting one form of expression for another: this may be called an analysis of our forms of expressions, for the process is sometimes like one of taking things apart." [24] We saw Ryle using this method in the example about carnivorous cows.

Another method employed by Wittgenstein and philosophical

[20] A. G. N. Flew, "Philosophy and Language," in *Essays in Conceptual Analysis,* edited by A. G. N. Flew (London: Macmillan & Co., Ltd., 1956), p. 4; first published in the *Philosophical Quarterly,* Vol. 5 (1955).

[21] J. Xenakis, "Ordinary-Language Philosophy," in *Synthese,* Vol. II (1959); see also P. Strawson, "On Referring," in *Mind,* Vol. 59 (1950).

[22] Flew, *op. cit.,* p. 12.

[23] M. Weitz, "Oxford Philosophy," in *Philosophical Review,* Vol. 62 (1953), p. 229.

[24] *Philosophical Investigations,* p. 43e.

analysts in order to get at the logic of ordinary language and resolve philosophical confusions has become known as the "argument of the paradigm case." Wittgenstein gives us this example: some questions are like asking the length of the standard-meter in Paris. Some think that because we can ask the length of this or that piece of metal we can also ask for the length of the standard-meter. This is absurd, because "length" means being measured against the standard-meter. The standard-meter is "something with which comparison is made," a paradigm in a particular language-game.[25] Philosophical confusions similar to asking for the length of the standard-meter arise through not observing paradigms in language-games. Flew goes so far as to say that "the clue to the whole business" of getting at the logic of language lies in mastering the argument of the paradigm case, describing the method with this example: ". . . if there is any word the meaning of which can be taught by reference to paradigm cases, then no argument whatever could ever prove that there are no cases of whatever it is. Thus, since the meaning of 'of his own free will' can be taught by reference to such paradigm cases as that in which a man, under no social pressure, marries the girl he wants to marry . . . : it cannot be right, on any grounds whatsoever, to say that no one *ever* acts of his own free will." [26] The free will-determinism issue is really a pseudo-problem which turns on the misuse of concepts, and logical analysis (attention to paradigm cases) resolves the problem. Attention to such cases shows us that "it is not contradictory to say that some act was both predictable and performed of the agent's own free will." [27]

Logical analysis, it is argued, also resolves the traditional debate over the subjectivity or objectivity of ethical concepts. Many traditional philosophers were bewitched by the Fido-Fido theory of meaning, the view that a word must name or describe in order to be meaningful. In moral philosophy, this "logical dogma," as Nowell-Smith calls it,[28] or "descriptive fallacy," as Professor Austin calls it,[29] generates philosophical confusions, including the claim of the posi-

[25] *Philosophical Investigations,* p. 25e.
[26] Flew, *op. cit.,* p. 19.
[27] *Ibid.,* p. 13.
[28] P. H. Nowell-Smith, *Ethics* (London: Unwin Brothers, Ltd., 1954), pp. 61-62.
[29] "Other Minds," in *Logic and Language,* p. 146.

tivist that moral concepts are pseudo-concepts and meaningless, and the claim of Moore and the ethical intuitionists that they refer to "nonnatural" qualities. We must not be misled by grammar—by the fact that "good" is used as a grammatical predicate—to the assumption that "good" must designate a quality similar to "yellow." What we must do is examine our actual linguistic usage and see how value words function. When we do this, Nowell-Smith points out, we find that value words have a number of functions. They express choices or decisions. They are used to instruct, command, advise, exhort, and praise. These roles or uses are often quite different from the roles or uses of descriptive words. The request, "What does the word 'good' (or 'right') stand for?" is, then, often a misplaced request, for these concepts are often not used to refer at all. They have unique meanings all their own based on different functions from that of naming. Even the way in which "reasons" support value judgments is different from the way in which reasons are related to descriptions, and we must not be misled into accepting the deductive model as the only model.[30] Value language and ethical reasoning have their own "logic," and the analytic philosopher, it is claimed, in reminding us of this logic, resolves the pseudo-problems (subjective-objective controversy) often associated with ethics.

Analytic philosophers have, in fact, turned their attention to a whole host of traditional philosophical problems with a view to "dissolving" them. Professor Strawson has analyzed the puzzle over the concept of truth. This puzzle is rooted in the assumption (made by Tarki, Carnap, and others) that the function of "true" in sentences must be descriptive, that "to say that a statement is true is to make a statement about a sentence of a given language, viz., the language in which the first statement was made." [31] Strawson argues that "the phrase 'is true' is not applied to sentences; for it is not applied to anything. Truth is not a property of symbols; for it is not a property." [32] The function of "true" is "confirmatory," not

[30] S. Toulmin, *An Examination of the Place of Reason in Ethics* (Cambridge: Cambridge University Press, 1950), p. 82.

[31] P. Strawson, "Truth," in *Analysis,* Vol. 9 (1948-49); reprinted in *Philosophy and Analysis,* edited by Margaret Macdonald (New York: Philosophical Library, Inc., 1955), p. 261.

[32] *Ibid.,* p. 262.

descriptive. The function of "true" is like the function of "yes" when one replies to a question.

Professor Findlay has applied the technique of analysis to the problem of time,[33] Professor Edwards and others to the problem of induction,[34] Professor Paul to the problem of perception and the sense datum theory,[35] Professor Hart to various issues in legal philosophy,[36] Professor Austin to the concept of knowledge,[37] Professors Macdonald, Weldon, and Berlin to problems in political theory,[38] and so on. Many agree that the results of these analyses have been quite fruitful, that in fact the analytic technique has made possible the settlement of many philosophical controversies. Others are more skeptical, offering strong criticisms of the techniques employed by the analysts.[39] Several have commented specifically on the limitations of the paradigm case method;[40] others that philosophy has reduced itself to grammaticism, philology, or lexicography. We are not concerned in this book with an evaluation of analytic philosophy. Such a task would be a long and difficult piece of work. We want here simply to describe the principal components of analytic philosophy. This in itself is not easily done, for most analysts are unwilling to be grouped into a school which holds certain basic tenets. There is no question that many of the analysts differ in techniques employed and often in their conclusions. There is, however, a great deal in common among the contemporary philosophical analysts.

[33] "Time, a Treatment of Some Puzzles," in *Logic and Language,* edited by A. Flew (Oxford: Basil Blackwell & Mott, Ltd., 1951).

[34] "Russell's Doubts About Induction," in *Ibid.*

[35] "Is There a Problem About Sense-Data?" in *Ibid.*

[36] "The Ascription of Responsibility and Rights," in *Ibid*; and "Natural Rights," *Philosophical Review,* Vol. 64 (1955).

[37] "Other Minds," in *Logic and Language,* Second Series (Oxford: Blackwell, 1953).

[38] "The Language of Political Theory," in *Logic and Language,* First Series (Oxford, 1951); T. D. Weldon, *The Vocabulary of Politics* (London: C. Nichols and Co., Ltd., 1953); and I. Berlin, "Equality," in *Aristotelian Society Proceedings,* Vol. 56 (1955-56).

[39] See Ernest Gellner, *Words and Things: A Critical Account of Linguistic Philosophy and a Study in Ideology* (London: Victor Gollancz Ltd., 1959).

[40] See A. Flew, "Philosophy and Language," in *Essays in Conception Analysis,* p. 20; and Robert Richman, "On the Argument of the Paradigm Case," in *The Australasian Journal of Philosophy,* Vol. 39, no. 1 (1961).

These common grounds are clearly seen in the prevalence of what Urmson calls "two new slogans": (1) Don't ask for the meaning, ask for the use, and (2) Every statement has its own logic.[41] Most contemporary analysts reject the logical positivist's account of meaning, not in its entirety, but as a total and adequate account of all meaning. The positivists are entirely too arbitrary in ruling out certain kinds of utterances as nonsense, meaningless, or purely emotive. A more fruitful approach, it is claimed, is a careful examination of the uses, functions, and purposes of language, since language is used to perform a variety of functions. The slogan that every statement has its own logic has the effect of making one look carefully at these various functions, thereby avoiding the error of the logical atomists that language has one essential function, that of picturing reality. It also has the effect of making us recognize that concepts and statements which have different uses or functions may be supported by reasons in radically different ways. In part at least, awareness of supporting reasons, the manner in which they support, and the situations for which they are devised, is awareness of the "logic" of whatever kind of statement is in question.

Furthermore, the conception of analysis as a reduction of the world to its basic indubitable constituents is for the most part abandoned.[42] The whole notion of the formation of an ideal language, generally associated with such an attempted reduction, is rejected. The attempt to construct a symbolic system or artificial language, much as does the formalist Carnap in *Der Logische Aufbau der Welt* or as does Bertrand Russell, is rejected in favor of looking for the "informal logic" of concepts and statements in the contexts of their use. The distinction between formal and informal logic is in fact widely accepted today, Professor Strawson being heavily responsible for its acceptance.[43] Contemporary analysts also emphasize that philosophical clarification can be achieved by means other than the translation or substitution method. This method is not rejected, but other techniques, such as the paradigm case method, are stressed.

There are, then, some key common elements in contemporary

[41] Urmson, *op. cit.*, p. 179.

[42] *Ibid.*, p. 186.

[43] P. Strawson, *Introduction to Logical Theory* (London: Methuen & Co., Ltd., 1952); and "On Referring," *op. cit.*

philosophical analysis. We have indicated that the methods of these analysts have been applied in a number of areas of discourse. Only recently, however, have philosophical analysts turned their attention to the language of religion. The positivists had simply dismissed religion and theology as a whole, or neatly placed it in the realm of the noncognitive. Contemporary analysts, however, are beginning to examine in great detail theological concepts and religious utterances. Religious discourse does in fact puzzle a number of people. The analyst attempts to rid us of these puzzles and help us understand religious language. Efforts have not been directed toward a translation of religious statements into equivalent statements—the method of substitution. Emphasis, for the most part, has been in the direction of trying to understand religious claims by examining in detail the entire context of religious discourse, the way in which religious utterances function, the various kinds of religious utterances, the specific situations which appear to call for a religious utterance, the sort of reasons adduced as supporting these utterances, and the manner in which they support. Awareness of all these factors is equivalent to awareness of the "logic" of religious discourse.

A comment of Stephen Toulmin perhaps best characterizes the modern analyst's attitude toward religion. He states:

> It is only if we suppose that religious arguments pretend (say) to provide exact knowledge of the future—so competing with science on its own ground—that we can be justified in attempting to apply to them the logical criteria appropriate to scientific explanations; and only if we do this that we have any grounds for concluding (with Ayer) that "all utterances about the nature of God are non-sensical" or (with Freud) that religion is "an illusion." Provided that we remember that religion has functions other than that of competing with science and ethics on their own grounds, we shall understand that to reject all religious argument for this reason is to make a serious logical blunder—an error as great as that of taking figurative phrases literally, or of supposing that the mathematical theory of numbers (say) has any deep religious significance.[44]

[44] S. Toulmin, *op. cit.*, pp. 212-213.

There is little question that the method of doing philosophy which we have described above, often characterized as "linguistic analysis" (and by some as "one of the greatest achievements of modern philosophy" [45]) is in part responsible for the current revival of interest in theology and religion. Philosophical analysts, in the words of Hook, provided a "method which could be employed both to clarify theological usage and to preserve its autonomy against 'rude' requests from scientists and naturalists to talk sense as defined by the parochial criteria of the scientific and common-sensical mode of discourse. There is not a single language-game that can be laid down in advance as binding upon all who would speak. . . ." [46] The slogan "Every statement has its own logic" has left philosophers and theologians free to look for and discover the logic peculiar to the religious mode of discourse. This is what Toulmin is suggesting that we do. Many have been looking. Some have been skeptics, others believers. These analysts have come up with alternative and conflicting conclusions concerning the logic of religious discourse. All of them, I think, have shed some light on this complex type of discourse. We will examine in some detail the efforts of a number of prominent philosophical analysts who have concentrated attention on the language of religion in two later chapters.

[45] W. B. Gallie, "The Function of Philosophical Aesthetics," in *Aesthetics and* Language, edited by W. Elton (Oxford: Basil Blackwell & Mott, Ltd., 1954), p. 22.

[46] Sidney Hook, "Preface," pp. xii-xiii, in *Religious Experience and Truth,* edited by Sidney Hook (New York: New York University Press, 1961).

CHAPTER FOUR

Defining "Religious Belief"

We have stated that we must be able to set boundaries for statements or beliefs that are religious, even if those boundaries are not entirely clear. Having such boundaries, one can distinguish statements and beliefs which are religious from statements and beliefs of other kinds. Performing this task is logically prior to deciding whether religious beliefs have cognitive meaning and whether they constitute knowledge. We turn then to a consideration of what makes a statement or belief religious.

In a recent article, E. D. Klemke states that he will take as religious all kinds of statements which are "found within the Christian faith," though, of course, he recognizes that there are religions other than Christianity.[1] He classifies these sentences as to kinds, and proceeds to ask if they are verifiable or falsifiable. Commands or exhortations like "Thou shalt not take the name of the Lord Thy God in vain" or "Love one another" are characterized as religious. Blessings such as "Grace to you and peace from God our Father and the Lord, Jesus Christ" are taken as religious. Questions like "Whence cometh my help?" are described as religious. Ejaculations such as "Woe is me, wretched man that I am" are also so described. Many sentences which *appear* to *assert* something are also characterized as religious. Examples that Klemke cites are "The Lord is my shepherd" and "Faith moves mountains." These religious sentences are not to be interpreted literally. Other religious sentences are

[1] E. D. Klemke, "Are Religious Statements Meaningful?", in *The Journal of Religion,* vol. 41 (1960).

actually assertive, and are to be taken literally. These include descriptive religious sentences like "Many Christians pray" or "X believes the assertions of the Apostles' Creed." Other religious sentences are explanations and can be tested for validity, for example, "The lack of rain in X is due to the people's sinfulness." Some religious sentences, Klemke tells us, are historical claims. "Jesus was born in Bethlehem," "The apostle Paul was imprisoned," and "Jesus healed paralytics instantaneously" are examples. Some religious sentences are autobiographical statements, for example, "I am convinced that Christ died for me." A final group of religious sentences, including "God exists," "Jesus is the son of God," and "God loves us," are the most perplexing group to Klemke. These sentences purport to be assertive, but they cannot be tested as can the religious sentences denominated as descriptive, explanatory, historical, or autobiographical. In spite of this lack of testability, the religious man insists that they are true.

Klemke maintains, then, that the class of religious sentences includes commands or exhortations, blessings, questions, ejaculations, statements not to be taken literally, descriptions, explanations, historical statements, autobiographical statements, and sentences which purport to assert but which cannot be tested. Klemke, I think, is correct that the class of religious sentences includes all these different types of sentences. Such a classification, however, does not provide us with a criterion for distinguishing religious sentences from other kinds of sentences. Professor Klemke does not concern himself directly with such a criterion, but it does seem clear that many of the sentences which he denominates as religious might not be called religious at all on certain occasions. Is the belief or statement that Jesus was born in Bethlehem a religious one? It need not be. True, this is a historical assertion concerning the major figure of a religion, but in many contexts it may not perform a religious function. The fact that a sentence is historical—even a historical statement about a central figure of a religion or about a feature of a religion—does not make that sentence religious. A nonreligious sentence can perform this function. Furthermore, descriptive sentences like "Many Christians pray" need not be viewed as specifically religious, although they describe facts about a religion. Nonreligious sentences can certainly perform this function. Similar remarks hold for commands or exhortations. "Love one another," for example, need not be viewed as specifically religious.

Our point is that the fact that a sentence is descriptive, explanatory, historical, autobiographical, or exhortative does not make it a religious sentence, although sentences which fall into any of these classes *may* be religious. What we need is a test or criterion for distinguishing religious sentences which are descriptive, explanatory, historical, autobiographical, or exhortative from nonreligious sentences which fall into these classes.

Can we find such a criterion? The activity of some philosophers of religion would indicate that we can. In fact, some philosophers seem to think that the term "religious" or "religion" designates some sort of essence. They continually ask for the *essence* of religion, and they search for a definition which captures that essence. Contemporary philosophical analysts, however, under the influence of Wittgenstein, warn us *not* to look for some essence as the meaning of a term. The view that the meaning of a word is an object, entity, or essence, and that to every word there corresponds a meaning is responsible for erroneous theories in all parts of philosophy. It makes the ethical theorist talk of nonnatural properties and subsistent entities, just as it made Plato speak of ideas or forms to provide meaning for terms like "man" and "justice." It is argued that the meaning of a term or phrase can be discovered simply by observing the use, function, or role of that term or phrase in language.

Suppose, then, that we accept the view that there is no essence which the term "religion" or "religious" designates. Suppose that we accept the Wittgensteinian position that the meaning of a term is the role or function or use of that term in language. Although in this view of meaning the term "religious" does not designate some sort of eternal, unchanging entity or essence, nonetheless this approach to meaning can provide us with a definition of religion or religious in terms of the characteristic role or function performed by sentences designated as religious. We are suggesting, then, that the test or criterion for whether a given belief or sentence is religious is whether that belief or sentence performs a given role or function in the language and lives of people, and that this role or function can be ascertained by examining the use of the term "religious" and the beliefs to which it is applied.

We will straightforwardly state the role or function which we think is characteristic of a religious belief. If a belief performs the function of providing an object (or objects) of devotion and an *all pervasive* frame of orientation, then it is religious. This criterion for the phrase "religious belief" has been suggested by several philosophers. Charles Morris in his *Signs, Language, and Behavior* remarks that "the complicated human self has need of some focal attitude to give it orientation, and the significance of religion lies in its attempt to meet this need." [2] Professor Morris suggests that this need for a focal attitude of orientation requires the formulation of a special type of discourse. Needs other than that of a focal attitude of orientation require other "specializations of common language." Each of these specializations of common language Professor Morris calls a "type of discourse." His suggestion is that the type of discourse centering around the need for some focal attitude to give the human self-orientation and the fulfillment of this need is religious discourse.

A view of religion and religious discourse similar to that of Professor Morris is held by Erich Fromm. Fromm defines religion as "any system of thought and action shared by a group which gives the individual a frame of orientation and an object of devotion." [3] The meaning of any sentence that is distinctly religious is always related to the function of providing a "frame of orientation and an object of devotion." The object or objects which perform this role may vary from time to time and place to place. What makes an object and statements about that object distinctly religious is *not* the fact that the object is the "supernatural," "God," "the Unmoved Mover," etc., or the fact that these statements refer to these or some quality of them, but rather it is the fact that this object and statements about it perform the function of providing what Fromm calls "a frame of orientation and an object (or objects) of devotion," or what Morris calls a "focal attitude of orientation." It is not necessarily true that an object—God, the supernatural, or the Unmoved

[2] Charles Morris, *Signs, Language, and Behavior* (Englewood Cliffs, N. J.: Prentice-Hall, Inc., 1946), p. 148.

[3] Erich Fromm, *Psychoanalysis and Religion* (New Haven: Yale University Press, 1950), p. 21.

Mover—and statements or beliefs about this object perform this function, and hence this object and statements or beliefs about it are not necessarily religious.

That statements are not religious simply because they contain certain specifiable words like "God" is clearly pointed out by William Kennick.[4] Kennick notes that Thales reportedly said that "all things are full of Gods," and Aristotle makes many statements containing the words "theos" and "theoi," but these statements have no religious significance. Many statements made about God, like Aristotle's proofs for the existence of the Prime Mover, are presumptive scientific statements. The fact, then, that statements contain words like "God," "Unmoved Mover," "Jesus," "creation," and "soul" does not necessarily mean that those statements are religious ones, although any statement with one of these words in it (or a host of other words) *may* be a religious statement. A statement or belief is religious or it becomes religious, we are suggesting, if it fulfills the role or function of providing a *focal* attitude of orientation and object or objects of devotion (or is a reflection of that attitude).

Kennick makes two further points concerning the attempt to define "religious statement." First, he points out that it has been held that religious statements are to be distinguished from other types of statements by the *natures* of the different objects concerned or referred to. Both St. Thomas and Aristotle talked about "higher" and "lower" sciences, the former dealing with higher and more noble objects. Aside from the fact that this distinction involves value judgments (and, of course, metaphysics) and consequently the problems of justifying those value judgments, it is probable that the distinction between higher and lower begs the question of what is religious as opposed to what is nonreligious. That a statement or belief is religious is made an analytic entailment of its being about a higher and nobler object. Kennick correctly points out that this distinction between higher and lower objects, as a means of distinguishing the religious statement from the nonreligious, simply "removes the difficulty from religious words to religious objects, and we may rightly ask whether there are any objects (or 'beings') which

[4] William Kennick, "The Language of Religion," *Philosophical Review,* vol. 65 (January, 1956).

are inherently religious." [5] If we are correct in our contention that what makes an object or statements and beliefs about that object (or objects) religious is the fact that it provides a focal attitude of orientation and an object of devotion, then no given object is *necessarily* a religious one, and any given object *may* be religious if it fulfills this function. Granted that once the distinction between higher and lower objects is made and certain statements or beliefs are held about the former, there is a high probability that that object and statements or beliefs about it are religious. This is because that higher and nobler object and the statements or beliefs about it have one's total commitment and provide a focal attitude of orientation and object of devotion.

Secondly, Kennick points out that another criterion that has been suggested for distinguishing religious from nonreligious statements is the literalness of the latter and the analogicity of the former. We will discuss the problems confronting the doctrine of analogical predication in detail in the next chapter. The only point we wish to make here, in agreement with Kennick, is that analogicity will not serve as a necessary and sufficient condition for distinguishing religious from nonreligious statements. Although many religious statements are set forth as analogical, this is also true of many nonreligious statements.

Professor Kennick's own criterion for distinguishing religious from nonreligious statements agrees with the one we are advocating, the position of Professor Morris and that of Erich Fromm. He says, for example, that "an attitude's being religious seems to be a function of its proportion or what we might call its 'weight.' If it assumes a vital, and above all, *pervasive* role in the life of a man or of a society, conditioning, determining, and focusing all or most other attitudes and reactions—those which have as their objects the natural world, cultural institutions, and other men and other societies, and even, or perhaps especially, those attitudes which a man takes toward himself—then we may properly call such an attitude or group of attitudes 'religious.' " [6] This is precisely what we mean by

[5] *Ibid.*, p. 58.
[6] *Ibid.*, p. 68.

a belief's providing a focal attitude of orientation and object or objects of devotion.

Now admittedly our test of a statement's being religious (fulfillment of the function cited above) lets a number of beliefs and statements in the door as being religious. The tenets of Marxism, Nazism, Fascism, or Democracy, if they performed the function described, would be viewed as religious. This means that there are not certain definite beliefs which are compatible with being religious and other beliefs which are definitely incompatible with being religious. The belief, for example, that Christ existed as a historical person may not provide a focal attitude of orientation and object of devotion in one's life, and hence need not be a religious belief. This belief, however, may perform this function in the life of another person, and hence be a religious belief for that person. On the other hand, the belief in determinism is not incompatible with being religious, in spite of the fact that some people think that it is. The belief in determinism fulfilled in Spinoza's life the function of providing a focal attitude of orientation, and hence that belief was religious to him.

The broad definition of religious, religious belief, or religious statement that we have been using has a number of advantages. First, it avoids a narrow, conventional, or provincial view of religion which arbitrarily rules out as religious any beliefs except those of a small specified group. One finds this narrow conception of religion quite often in the conversations of lay people. As William Christian notes, they often set forth a persuasive definition of religion, as opposed to a general or generic one, in remarks like "religion holds that . . ." or "religion believes that . . ." or "religion teaches that. . . ." [7] The suggestion is that one is not *really* religious unless one supports whatever is put in the blanks. Quite clearly, such remarks are made to get one to adopt some particular religious belief.

A more specific example of a persuasive definition of "religion" is that of Albert C. Knudson. Knudson maintains that the phrase "Godless religion" is a self-contradictory phrase. "To give up the

[7] William A. Christian, "Some Varieties of Religious Belief," in *Review of Metaphysics,* vol. 4 (1950), p. 597.

belief . . . in divine providence is to turn over to the enemy the innermost citadel of religious faith."[8] Knudson is defending a certain form of theism, and his remarks, in the context of a discussion about naturalistic humanism, are made to deny the possibility of naturalistic humanism's being a religious position. Persuasive definitions of this sort do not contribute to clarity. In fact, they promote a great deal of confusion, often cutting off communication. Other examples of persuasive definitions of religion which tend to stop inquiry and communication are those set forth by Marxists, Freudians, and some Positivists. By identifying religious beliefs with supernaturalistic beliefs, and by categorizing all supernaturalistic beliefs as mere "expressions of emotion," "projections of desires," or "opiates which assist the bourgeois," religion and religious beliefs come to be viewed as matters about which no further decisions are called for.[9]

Our objection, of course, is that the phrases "religious belief" and "belief in the supernatural" are not at all equivalent, although the latter may on occasion fall into the class of religious belief. Furthermore, such narrow conceptions of religion or religious belief often beg the question, building the conclusion that one wants into the definition of religion with which one begins. Our wider conception of religion or religious statements, which denies that there are certain beliefs which are essential to being religious (the belief in a transcendent God, for example) and that other beliefs are always incompatible with being religious, has the advantage of not restricting discussion and of avoiding question-begging techniques.

The extreme disadvantage of a narrow, persuasive definition of religion, one which reflects one's own personal religious beliefs, can be seen more clearly by making an analogy with ethical theory. One finds that, in the history of ethical theory, a given definition of "ethical" is often simply a reflection of a set of normative ethical beliefs. For example, Jeremy Bentham makes the following statement: "Of an action that is conformable to the principle of utility, one may always say either that it is one that ought to be done, or at

[8] Albert C. Knudson, *Basic Issues in Christian Thought* (Nashville, Tenn.: Abingdon-Cokesbury Press, 1950), p. 28; quoted by Christian, *op. cit.*

[9] William A. Christian, *op. cit.*, p. 598; Christian (616) sets forth a definition of "religious belief" which is very similar to the one we are advocating.

least that it is not one that ought not to be done. . . . When thus interpreted the words *ought* and *right* and *wrong,* and others of that stamp, have a meaning: When otherwise, they have none." [10]

One interpretation of this passage is that Bentham's commitment to the principle of utility has led him here to assert the thesis that the normative terms "ought," "right," etc. could *mean* nothing other than that specified by the utilitarian. His thesis is one about the meaning of ethical terms, not so much a thesis about what we ought to do. But it is clear that his position in normative ethics—that we should act so as to increase the happiness and welfare of all people—is the foundation or source for his definition of "ethical." His definition of "ethical" and his preclusion of other definitions is a consequence of his acceptance of the normative ethical views of utilitarianism. He has so defined the ethical that an act *must* conform to the principle of utility to be an ethical act.

However, a definition or account of the meaning of "ethical" need not be a reflection of one's ethical evaluations. The ethical, or terms like "ought" and "right," could be defined in terms of *use* and *function*—in a morally neutral manner. A morally neutral account of such concepts would be the result of an analysis of the features and functions of discourse in which these terms are used. One discovers the features and functions by examining the use. Thus, Nowell-Smith offers an account of the meaning of ethical concepts in terms of the uses or functions which they perform. Following Wittgenstein, he substitutes for the question "What does the word x mean?" two questions: "For what job is the word x used?" and "Under what conditions is it proper to use this word for that job?" [11] Certain words and adjectives exhibit a great variety of "logical behaviour," and Nowell-Smith finds it necessary to distinguish several different uses which words and adjectives have, including aptness-use, gerundive-use, and descriptive-use. A given adjective, such as "good" or "right," may mean different things on different occasions depending on its use or role, and this use or role

[10] Jeremy Bentham, *The Principles of Morals and Legislation* (London, 1789); reprinted in part in *Ethical Theories,* second edition edited by A. I. Meldon (Englewood Cliffs, N. J.: © Prentice-Hall, Inc., 1955), p. 344.

[11] P. Nowell-Smith, *Ethics* (London, 1954), p. 69.

can be discovered only be examining it in the context of its use. Conclusions from an analysis such as Nowell-Smith's would apply equally to the normative ethical concepts of Nietzsche, Kant, Mill, St. Paul, and Hitler, and would not be a reflection of a given normative ethic.

We are suggesting that just as ethical concepts can be defined in terms of use and function in a morally neutral manner, so also the words "religion," or "religious belief," can be defined in terms of use and function in a neutral manner (in a manner such that this definition is not a reflection of one's personal religious views). Such a conception of "religion" or "religious sentence" is the one we are advocating. Without a detailed analysis of discourse in which the terms "religion" and "religious" are used (a task beyond our present scope), we suggest that if a belief or statement fulfills the function of providing a focal attitude of orientation and an object or objects of devotion, then that belief or statement is religious. This account of the meaning of "religion" or "religious statement" is neutral to all religious beliefs in the sense that it is not a reflection of anyone's personal religious views.

We may now summarize our conclusions. We have argued that a religious belief or sentence can be distinguished from beliefs or sentences of other kinds in terms of the characteristic use or function performed. We have suggested that the characteristic use or function performed by a religious sentence or belief is that of providing a focal attitude of orientation and an object (or objects) of devotion. Religious beliefs are to be viewed as those beliefs which play an all-pervasive role in the life of a man, a group, or culture, determining most of the attitudes and reactions of that man, that group, or that culture. Beliefs performing this all-pervasive function will vary and do vary from time to time, place to place, man to man, group to group, and culture to culture. Obviously there will be many borderline cases, cases of beliefs which approximate this all-pervasive function but which are difficult to classify as religious or nonreligious. Furthermore, beliefs which perform this function on one occasion may not on another. This fact is a result of our defining "religious belief" in terms of use and function, and our denying that there is some sort of essence designated by the terms "religion" or "religious belief." Nonetheless, we do have a rough criterion by which to distinguish religious beliefs from beliefs of other kinds. It is only with a prior criterion in mind for the phrase "religious belief" or "religious sentence" that one can significantly proceed to ask if religious beliefs are either cognitive or true.

CHAPTER FIVE

The Problem of Cognitivity

The Issue of Cognitive Significance

Thus far we have argued for a definition of "religious" or "religious belief" which is neutral to any specific religious beliefs. Let us now concentrate our attention on the question of whether religious sentences are cognitive (capable of being true or false). We have already noted that this question is logically prior to the question of whether religious sentences or claims constitute knowledge.

A number of contemporary philosophers have argued that religious utterances (specifically, claims about the nature and existence of a transcendent God) are noncognitive expressions of emotion.[1] These utterances, it is argued, do not assert anything which *could* be true or false. This contention seems quite paradoxical since the behavior and reactions of persons making these religious claims indicate that they intend (on many occasions, but not all) their utterances as cognitive—disputable perhaps, but at least capable of being true or false. The emotivist's contention is also paradoxical in the light of the fact that religious utterances are often understood by the hearer to be asserting something. Furthermore, religious language makes use of all the modes of speech characteristic of cognitive discourse. That is, there is considerable linguistic evidence which prima facie supports a cognitive interpretation of reli-

[1] See, for example, A. J. Ayer, *Language, Truth, and Logic* (London, 1946).

gious discourse[2]—specifically a cognitive interpretation of statements or claims about God.

First of all, religious discourse about God often takes the form of indicative sentences just as do other sentences known to be cognitive. Is this not prima facie evidence that religious utterances are cognitive? That is, if these religious claims are simply expressions of emotion, commands, or interjections, why do they not take the form of commands or interjections?

It is possible that the indicative form of religious utterances is an accident of our language, but since such utterances also take the indicative form in other languages, this is unlikely. Certainly, the fact that they take this form cannot be dismissed as having no import. However, the fact that an utterance takes the indicative form is surely not a necessary and sufficient condition for its cognitivity. The positivist is quick to point out that we are often misled by the "surface grammar" of our language. Quite often, for example, sentences that take the indicative form are commands, not assertions. For example, the sentence "John is going home!" is quite often used to command, not describe. Nonetheless, the fact that religious utterances often take the indicative form is prima facie evidence for a cognitive interpretation of those utterances. Surely some detailed explanation is required if one is to interpret them as simply expressions of emotion, commands, or interjections.

A second kind of linguistic evidence that claims about God are cognitive is found by looking at religious questions. Questions like "Is God really a just God?" indicate that the speaker is asking for an answer that can be true or false. If claims about God were purely emotive utterances, then questions of this kind would hardly be appropriate.

However, does the fact that religious discourse includes questions which appear to require answers which can be true or false *prove* that religious utterances are cognitive? No. It does show that they are *intended* to be cognitive. But surely some explanation must be given to this fact about language if the emotive interpretation of religious discourse is to be justified.

[2] Peter Glassen ("The Cognitivity of Moral Judgments," in *Mind,* vol. 66, no. 269 (January, 1959) cites similar linguistic evidence in support of a cognitive interpretation of *moral* judgments.

A third fact which tends to support a cognitive interpretation of sentences about God is that religious utterances often appear in indirect discourse as the object of a cognitional verb, like "know" or "believe." For example, one quite often finds judgments like "I know that God is a just God," or "I believe that God is a just God." Here religious utterances are indirectly referred to as objects of cognitions. This is pretty clear evidence that when ordinary people make religious utterances they often intend to say something cognitive and are quite often understood as having done so. But if the emotive interpretation of these utterances is true, then they *can* carry no cognitive meaning. Utterances like "I believe there is a just God" must be viewed as expressing commands or feelings. The plain man who makes such utterances must be shown that he isn't really saying anything which *could* be known. This, of course, seems paradoxical to the religious person who obviously intends to say something cognitive when making these religious claims.

A fourth kind of evidence for the cognitive interpretation of religious discourse is that appraisal terms like "correct" or "mistaken" and "true" or "false" are applied to religious utterances. Thus, we find persons saying, "It is a mistake to think of God as transcendent," or "The Christian conception of God is the true one." This is further evidence that in ordinary discourse these religious utterances are intended to convey cognitive meaning. Again, if the emotive view is correct, it must explain why in ordinary religious discourse both the addressee and the addressor intend their remarks to be cognitive but are misled in doing so. The emotivist must show that both parties to a religious dispute are disagreeing in *attitude* but not in *belief*.

The above four characteristics of religious language and its use show that religious discourse often makes use of all the modes of speech characteristic of debates in which there is disagreement in belief, and hence this discourse *appears* to be cognitive. A justification of the emotive interpretation requires an explaining away of these facts about religious discourse. The emotivist must show that although people intend to make cognitive assertions in religious discourse and are understood as doing so, and although in religious discourse all the modes of speech characteristic of cognitive discourse are used, what really occurs is the expressing of an attitude and perhaps the attempt to alter the attitude of one's opponent.

On what grounds can the emotive interpretation of religious discourse be justified? Generally the justifying ground for this interpretation of religious utterances is a particular criterion of cognitive meaning which dictates what sorts of cognitive statements there can be. We have seen that noncognitivists in regard to claims about a transcendent God have generally based their views on the empirical verifiability criterion of meaning, arguing that there can only be two kinds of cognitive sentences—empirical or contingent propositions, and analytic or necessary propositions. Since religious utterances about God are not set forth as analytic or tautological, and since they appear not to be contingent in the sense that some empirical data *could* in principle verify them, it is argued that religious utterances must really be emotive utterances. They are expressive of certain sorts of attitudes, but are noncognitive.

We have seen, however, that this treatment of religious claims —this deduction of the cognitive meaninglessness of religious and theological statements from the verifiability criterion—is now generally recognized as arbitrary and inadequate even by those within the general positivist and empiricist tradition. In fact, this dismissal of religious, theological, and metaphysical statements as meaningless, without a careful examination of the particulars of each claim, has been recognized as a procedure which, in a real sense, is against the tenor of empiricism as a methodological approach.

On what grounds, then, can we ascertain whether religious statements have cognitive or empirical meaning? Can we decide this by looking at the use and users of language and by discovering what sorts of utterances are commonly used by speakers to assert something and are commonly understood as asserting something by those who are addressed? When we do this—when we look at the use and users of religious language—we find that claims about God often fall into the class of utterances which are intended by speakers to assert something capable of being true or false, and which are also understood as such by the hearer. Most of these utterances are not intended by the speaker to be simply expressions of emotion or commands. Nor are they understood as such by the hearer. This is shown by the four kinds of evidence cited above.

However, does this evidence from language prove that religious utterances *are* cognitive? Certainly it proves that religious utterances are often *intended* to be cognitive. That they are so intended is prima facie evidence that they are cognitive, but these data are not necessary and sufficient evidence. One could intend to say something cognitive but not really assert anything. Since this is the case, there is no necessary relationship between one's intending a sentence to be cognitive and that sentence being cognitive. Nor is there a necessary relationship between one's being understood as asserting something and one's really asserting something. Both the addressee and the addressor could simply be deriving psychological satisfaction from sentences which are nonassertive or sentences which have been emptied of their factual content. The evidence cited above, then, does not *prove* the cognitivity of religious utterances.

What we need is a means of testing whether any given religious sentence is *really* cognitive, as opposed to its being *intended* as cognitive. One can do this only by ascertaining whether or not the sentence conforms to a standard or to criteria for cognitivity, and that standard itself is not ascertainable by purely empirical means. Any criterion or set of criteria of cognitive meaning functions as a norm and is devised to provide this test, and the issue of justifying such a criterion is that, at least in part, of justifying a norm. Cognitivity is not something that wears its face on the surface of things in such a way that it can be discovered simply by looking for it. That is, the issue of cognitivity is not a purely descriptive issue at all. The phrase "cognitively meaningful" is partially normative, and a judgment that a particular utterance is cognitively meaningful is very much like an evaluative judgment in ethics. It amounts to saying that we ought to treat that judgment as being capable of truth or falsity, and we should so treat it because it conforms to an accepted standard or norm for cognitivity.

This norm or standard of cognitivity is confronted with difficulties similar to those that arise in justifying an ethical principle. A justification requires that one give supporting reasons. But what is a good reason for adopting a given criterion or set of criteria for cognitive meaning? Is the fact that a given criterion of cognitive meaning "eliminates metaphysics" and directs the attention of philosophers to something "more important" a good reason for adopting that criterion? Certainly not for some thinkers. Is the fact that a criterion of cognitive meaning "provides the framework for a general theoretical account of the structure and the foundations of scientific knowledge" [3] a good reason for adopting that criterion? Many thinkers, theologians in particular, would argue that this is not a good reason for adopting such a criterion, especially if that criterion rules out the possibility of religious meaning and knowledge. In a similar manner, many of the early positivists rejected their own early criterion of cognitivity upon recognizing the radical consequences which followed from it (a denial of the factual meaningfulness of the major part of science). Certainly the reasons that have been offered in support of the empirical verifiability criterion of meaning have been pragmatic reasons. It has been pointed out that certain results, considered good and desirable (such as those cited above) or undesirable will accrue if one adopts that criterion of cognitive meaning. The issue of adopting such a criterion has not been treated as one which could be resolved on purely empirical or factual grounds.[4] Since the issue of choice of a criterion of cognitivity is neither an issue which can be settled empirically nor a conclusion which is logically coercive, but rather an issue to be resolved on pragmatic grounds, the religious advocate can certainly reject the positivist's criterion. He need only point out that what constitutes a good reason for adopting that criterion for the positivist is not a good reason for himself—given the goals and desiderata of religion.

Hempel's approach to the issue of cognitive significance is perhaps the least arbitrary and most liberal of those in the empiricist tradition. We have seen that he prefers to apply the phrase "cognitive significance" to "systems," and he maintains that different systems have different degrees of cognitive significance, the degree being determined by the extent to which statements or concepts constituting the system conform to four criteria: (1) the clarity and precision

[3] Carl G. Hempel, "Problems and Changes in the Empiricist Criterion of Meaning," in *Semantics and the Philosophy of Language,* edited by Leonard Linsky (Urbana: University of Illinois Press, 1952), p. 182; reprinted from *Revue Internationale de Philosophie,* II (1950).

[4] See Ayer, *op. cit.,* p. 16. Professor Ayer points out that Professor Ewing and Professor Stace wrongly interpret the empirical verifiability criterion of meaning as an empirical hypothesis.

of the theory, (2) formal simplicity, (3) the explanatory and predictive power of the system in regard to observable phenomena, and (4) the extent to which the theory has been confirmed by experimental evidence.[5] Hempel maintains that "speculative philosophical approaches," including, I think, metaphysics and theology, would make a poor showing on these tests. They would have a low degree of cognitive significance.

Now, to be sure, the religious advocate can reject the criteria for cognitive significance offered by Hempel. But clearly he himself must invoke, implicitly or explicitly, some criteria of his own. Although I know of no detailed attempt to apply Hempel's criteria to religious or theological systems, it is clear that many theologians who defend the factual status of religious claims appeal to criteria like these. They claim that theological concepts and statements have explanatory and predictive power in regard to observable phenomena and, further, that such statements are confirmed by empirical evidence. A liberal and modest test for factual meaningfulness accepted by a number of contemporary religious thinkers is the falsifiability test. This test requires only that some data be incompatible with a purported factual claim. If some data are incompatible with a given statement, then at least to some extent the reference range of that statement can be fixed. This being the case, both the speaker and hearer can know or find out, to some degree, what the statement is about and the extent of the claim being made. Such a test does not have the arbitrariness of the older verifiability criterion. Rather than a wholesale rejection of theological and metaphysical claims, this approach stresses a specific analysis of these claims, requiring only that some data be incompatible with any given claim.

Several comments must be made concerning the later Wittgenstein and Oxford philosophy in relation to the cognitivity issue. We have seen that the two principal slogans of this philosophical group are: "Don't ask for the meaning, ask for the use," and "Every statement has its own logic." These slogans were devised to make us realize that concepts and statements have many different uses, functions, or roles. The logic of religious statements is different from that of

[5] See Hempel, *op. cit.*

scientific statements. Religion "has functions other than that of competing with science and ethics on their own grounds. . . ." Our puzzlement over religious discourse and claims can be alleviated by examining religious statements in all their variety in the contexts in which they are used—in the context in which they perform their roles.

Now this approach to meaning has the distinct advantage of avoiding arbitrariness and the attempt to fit all statements into a few a priori categories. But it is not itself a solution to the question of whether religious statements have cognitive significance. To be sure, statements and concepts do perform many functions: descriptive, prescriptive, performatory, and expressive. But, having pointed this out, one must ask what function is performed by religious and theological statements. If religion does not compete with science, what does it do? The puzzlement over religious discourse might be alleviated by "discovering" (and some have "discovered" this) that religious discourse functions primarily not to communicate facts (cognitive function) but to express feelings. In order to decide this, however, some set of criteria for cognitive significance must be devised and applied to religious discourse. Simply to say that "meaning is use" or that "each type of statement has its own logic" does not answer the question. Nor can the question be answered simply by *describing* the uses of religious language. Some set of criteria for cognitive significance must be imposed, criteria which function as a standard or norm. We have suggested that a most modest test is the falsifiability test. This test is really a test for factual significance, but we also will loosely speak of it as a test of cognitivity since the kind of cognitive significance claimed for religious utterances is not formal but factual.[6]

Literal, Nonliteral, and Paradoxical Religious Sentences

We submit that there are many religious sentences or beliefs (beliefs which perform the function of providing a focal attitude of orientation and object or objects of devotion) which conform to the

[6] See chapter eight for a discussion of the distinction between formal and factual knowledge.

criterion of cognitivity (actually, the criterion of factual meaningfulness) which we have suggested. The beliefs, for example, that Christ lived and worked in Nazareth and that Christ was crucified, perform (along with a host of other related beliefs) for many people the function which we have designated as religious; and the speaker and hearer know or can find out what these statements are about and the extent of the claims being made. These sentences may also conform to the criteria (not yet suggested) for knowledge. The Marxist belief in dialectical materialism and the eventual attainment of ideal Communism is often set forth both as a descriptive and predictive sentence (though it may also be interpreted as an implicit normative contention or a metaphysical thesis), and it certainly performs a religious function. In this interpretation, the Marxist claim surely has cognitive significance, even though it might be disputable as a knowledge claim. The Nazi belief in a master race also performed a religious function, and can be interpreted so that it conforms to our criterion for cognitivity. The belief that Mohammed experienced a prophetic call and carried on a ministry in Mecca is a religious belief. This belief conforms to our criterion of cognitivity and, given some analysis of the phrase "prophetic call," may constitute knowledge.

Other beliefs which perform the function we have designated as religious include explanations like "The lack of rain is due to the people's sinfulness." Explanatory hypotheses of this sort can certainly be tested. Predictive sentences, like "Christ will return," perform a religious function, are testable according to a given set of criteria, and hence are cognitive. Other sentences which are importantly related to the function of providing a frame of orientation and object or objects of devotion are certain autobiographical statements. The sentence, for example, "I am positively sure that God is just" characterizes an attitude of conviction central to a given frame of orientation and object of devotion. Such sentences can certainly be tested by reference to autobiographical data. We need only check to see if a given person has the attitude of being positively sure, and there are criteria for discerning facts of this sort. The sentence, then, would be viewed as cognitive and may constitute knowledge.

Of course, there are sentences which fulfill the function designated as religious which are noncognitive or nonassertive. Ejaculations like "Woe is me, wretched man that I am!"; blessings like "Grace to you and peace from God our Father"; prayers like "Lord, have mercy upon me"; and commands like "Do not take the name of the Lord thy God in vain" all are expressive of feelings, feelings which in their usual context are related to a focal attitude of orientation and an object of devotion and hence fulfill a religious function. However, these sentences are not intended to be assertions that are true or false. In fact, most persons within a given religion would think it quite inappropriate to apply tests for truth or falsity to these sentences.

There are, then, religious sentences which are intended as cognitive and others which are not. Thus far we have pointed out cognitive religious sentences which we characterized as predictive, descriptive, historical, explanatory, and autobiographical. These sentences pose no particular problems for the philosophical analyst.

In fact, a whole host of key religious statements (such as "God exists," "God loves us," "Jesus is the son of God," "There is life after death," and "God created the world") can be and often are interpreted as predictive, descriptive, historical, explanatory, or autobiographical claims. On other occasions, however, these key religious claims are set forth in such a manner that they do *not* conform to the modes of verification or falsification to which predictive, descriptive, historical, explanatory, or autobiographical claims conform. In the latter case, these key religious claims give rise to serious problems.

Consider the sentence "God exists." Sometimes this sentence is taken as asserting that certain natural laws hold in the universe; on other occasions, that there is a purposive designer of the universe or that there is a first cause of all that exists. There are data relevant to testing these different interpretations of the sentence "God exists." Thus, the natural theologian[7] points to empirical evidence of design, to the existence of the cause and effect relationship in nature, and to the idea of God which he finds in his experience. It is now generally agreed that such evidence does not constitute proof of

[7] I do not want to identify theological sentences with religious sentences although the former may be, but certainly are not always, religious.

God's existence. The teleological argument faces all the problems pointed out by Hume. The cosmological and ontological arguments also confront numerous difficulties. However, although such data as cited by the natural theologian may not justify the claim of *knowledge* of God's existence, the sentence "God exists," when based on an appeal to this data, can certainly be labeled cognitive. It has data relevant to its truth or falsity even if the data are insufficient for a knowledge claim.

There is another interpretation of the meaning of the sentence "God exists," sometimes characterized as the "operational" view of God, in which there is no question of the cognitivity of this sentence. God is viewed as the source of values and as the "class of creative events." He is not transcendent, but is an event which functions in and among and through other spatio-temporal events. God is an order of events or a system of patterns. Admittedly, Wieman and other religious operationalists[8] need to be much clearer about the nature of this process or pattern of events which they identify with God. Wieman in particular, who speaks of God as the growth of meaning and value in the world, is not very clear. However, the meaning of the terms "growth" and "value" are on occasion specified in such a manner that one can grasp in part their meaning and recognize the kind of evidence relevant to the confirmation of the claim "God exists" or "There is growth of meaning and value in the world." That evidence is the existence of events characterized as having value. Here is a conception of God for which operational definitions can be given. Although this approach, when properly clarified, would bring joy to the hearts of many positivists, it is not, of course, the more ordinary conception of God or approach to knowledge of God. My own feeling is that Wieman's position is a disguised kind of naturalism.

The claim that God exists is also often held to rest upon a direct and immediate confrontation or experience of God. This evidence is generally referred to as "religious experience." The typical objection to religious experience as evidence that God exists is that such ex-

[8] See H. N. Wieman and W. M. Horton, *The Growth of Religion* (Chicago: Willett, Clark, & Co., 1938); and H. N. Wieman, "Can God be Perceived?" *Journal of Religion,* Vol. 23 (1943).

perience might be hallucinatory, that such data are not intersubjectively testable, and that one can never know if a given experience of God is veridical, i.e., is really an experience of God. However, since some data are relevant to the sentence "God exists," then that sentence, as interpreted by those who appeal to religious experience, can be viewed as cognitive, if the meaning of the sentence is construed as an autobiographical claim that one has had a given experience.

The sentence "God exists" is also often set forth as cognitive and true but it is denied that the empirical data cited by either the natural theologian or the data of religious experience are relevant to the truth or falsity of the sentence. The Barthians, for example, who insist that the use of the term "God" by the Biblical theologian is quite different from its use by the natural theologian, maintain that there is no way from the data of the world and human experience to God. John Smith[9] calls this the "discontinuity thesis," and points out that much current Protestant theology involves the denial of any rational way to God from either the cosmos or man's experience. Barth and his followers maintain that we know God neither through experience of natural objects nor through reason, but from the action in which God wills to make himself known (act of self-revelation). For Barth and neo-Protestant theology we have knowledge of God through his self-revelation in Jesus Christ. Christ represents the unique and only genuine revelation of God. In a sense, then, the Barthians do appeal to empirical data (the existence and behavior of Christ) as verifying data for God's existence and nature. We must, then, it seems to me, admit that the religious sentence "God exists" is cognitive as formulated by Barthians and others who point to the revelation of God in Christ as verifying data. But the problem is whether there is any way of testing a genuine revelation, distinguishing it from a spurious one, or of testing the view that Christ reveals God's nature and existence. Putting it more straightforwardly, the problem is whether the sentence "God exists," under this appeal, conforms to acceptable criteria for knowledge. (We shall see, however, that, to the extent that

[9] John Smith, "The Present Status of Natural Theology," in *The Journal of Philosophy,* Vol. 55, no. 22 (October 23, 1958), p. 926.

the doctrine of analogical predication is employed as a device for knowing God's nature through Christ's nature, serious problems concerning the cognitivity of statements about God arise again.)

If, however, the view that Christ is revelatory of God is interpreted to mean that Christ *is* God (doctrine of Incarnation), then fundamental problems concerning the cognitive significance of this claim arise. Some prominent religious thinkers maintain that the doctrine of the Incarnation and other key religious affirmations are paradoxical sentences. I am thinking of Emil Brunner and Soren Kierkegaard. What Brunner apparently means by paradoxical is "logical inconsistency." He states: "The hall-mark of logical inconsistency clings to all genuine pronouncements of faith." [10] "The natural man takes offense" at these religious claims, for "they are mysteries in which God reveals Himself as the Incomprehensible." [11] It is, of course, understandable that the "natural man" takes offense at these statements, since genuinely internally inconsistent statements are not meaningful. Statements of the form "X is the case and X is not the case," or statements in which one applies incompatible predicates to the same person or thing at the same time, do not impart information or communicate facts. As P. F. Strawson puts it, "Contradicting oneself is like writing something down and then erasing it, or putting a line through it. A contradiction cancels itself and leaves nothing." [12] Such use of language is certainly intolerable for one who expects language to perform an informative function. Paradoxical statements violate a fundamental requirement for using language informatively; and yet those who set forth paradoxical statements in religious discourse insist that those statements perform an informative function and that they are to be believed.

Now there is no serious problem with religious sentences which *appear* to be paradoxical in the above sense but which are not really paradoxical at all. We often use language in an apparently paradoxical manner in a number of areas of discourse. But these statements can be reformulated in nonparadoxical form. If, for example, someone asks you if you were pleased by something, you may reply: "Well,

[10] H. Emil Brunner, *Philosophy of Religion from the Standpoint of Protestant Theology* (2nd ed.) (London: James Clarke & Co., Ltd., 1958), p. 55.

[11] *Ibid.*, p. 96.

[12] P. F. Strawson, *Introduction to Logical Theory* (London, 1952), p. 3.

I was and I wasn't," and yet communicate perfectly well.[13] The statement has only the surface appearance of being paradoxical. Many statements which function religiously also have only the surface appearance of being internally inconsistent. They can be rephrased in nonparadoxical form. For example, the affirmation "Whoever would save his life will lose it" seems to be contradictory because, ordinarily, the term "save" contradicts what is meant by "lose." However, one nonparadoxical and meaningful interpretation of the sentence is that preoccupation with one's own life to the exclusion of others results in one's losing the ethical character of one's life.[14] The statement "The eternal mountains were scattered and the everlasting hills sank low" is also paradoxical if one views an eternal reality as that which cannot be altered. However, one meaningful and nonparadoxical interpretation of this sentence is that even mountains, which some men believe are eternal, will change.[15]

There is no serious problem, then, with religious sentences which appear to be internally inconsistent but which can be interpreted or rephrased in nonparadoxical language. However, there are religious claims which not only appear to be internally inconsistent but which admittedly cannot be reformulated in nonparadoxical language. As Brunner puts it, such statements are "incurably paradoxical." Kierkegaard calls such statements "absolute paradoxes."

Let's take an example. Speaking of the Incarnation, Brunner remarks that it is "the entrance into history of that which, by its very name, cannot enter into history, because it is eternal." [16] This statement is "incurably paradoxical." It is self-contradictory to assert that that which is eternal and cannot enter into history does in fact enter into history. This claim, for Brunner, cannot be reformulated into a nonparadoxical statement. If this is the case, then it seems clear that the question of believing the claim or the question of the truth or falsity of the claim cannot even arise; for it conveys nothing which *can* be believed. A contradiction cancels itself and leaves nothing. One cannot even speak of such sentences as making claims.

[13] *Ibid.*

[14] B. F. Kimpel, *Language and Religion* (New York: Philosophical Library, Inc., 1957), p. 113.

[15] *Ibid.*, p. 116.

[16] Emil Brunner, *The Mediator, a Study of the Central Doctrine of the Christian Faith* (Philadelphia: Westminster Press, 1947), p. 107.

The same problem confronts the "absolute paradox" which Kierkegaard talks about. That ". . . God has come into being, has been born, grown up, and so forth" [17] is a paradox which the religious believer is to accept. The claim is admittedly internally inconsistent, for God is defined as an eternal, unchanging reality. This is incompatible with God existing in human form and growing up. It would seem, then, that the sentence asserts nothing whatever. The issue of believing or not believing it does not arise, for the sentence violates a fundamental requirement for using language informatively. And unlike sentences which *appear* to be paradoxical but which can be rephrased in nonparadoxical form, this religious sentence is, for Kierkegaard, an "absolute paradox."

It is disturbing to find individuals, like Kierkegaard and Brunner, who do not require consistency in discourse and who seem not to be disturbed by a lack of it. To those of us who maintain that internal consistency is a fundamental requirement for the intelligible and informative use of language, such paradoxical language is intolerable. Such use of language simply does not communicate to many of us, though it seems to communicate to others. For my part such paradoxical sentences cannot be said to be either true or false because they have no cognitive significance. Most of us cannot emulate the example of the White Queen who could believe "three impossible things before breakfast." The possibility, however, of offering an interpretation of the Incarnation such that self-contradiction is not involved in the belief must be left open—this in spite of Brunner and (one interpretation of) Kierkegaard.

Brunner maintains that the philosopher or one who insists on the requirement of internal consistency and complete reliance upon reason is guilty of the sin of pride. This accusation, of course, is questionable. The view that God wants us to believe self-contradictions (even assuming that it makes sense to believe such) seems peculiar indeed. As one philosopher puts it, "It is no light thing to speak in the name of God, and, when the message is unintelligible [as in the case of paradoxical religious sentences], the philosopher shrewdly suspects that this unintelligibility is an indication, not of

[17] Soren Kierkegaard, *Concluding Unscientific Postscript,* translated by David Swenson, completed and edited by Walter Lowrie (Princeton: Princeton University Press, 1941). Second Printing, 1944, p. 188.

its divine origin, but of the muddle-headedness of the theologians who concocted it." [18]

Thus far we have seen that the religious sentence "God exists," as used by the natural theologian, by the religious operationalist, by those who appeal to religious experience, and by those who appeal to revelation through Christ can be so interpreted that there are conceivable and actual data relevant to its verification or falsification and hence that this sentence must be viewed as having factual meaning. Similar actual or possible evidence might be offered for other religious beliefs, such as "God loves us," "God created the world," "The soul survives the death of the body," etc., in which case these sentences must be denominated as cognitive. We have further argued that religious sentences which are "incurably paradoxical" (internally inconsistent) cannot be denominated as cognitive.

Some religious thinkers, however, including some theologians and some who appeal to revelation, maintain that God is transcendent and indescribable in human terms. Statements about God are not to be taken as *straightforward* empirical hypotheses or as literal truths, but as analogical truths or as symbolic truths. We turn now to a consideration of the doctrine of analogical predication and the view that religious statements are symbolically true.

The Doctrine of Analogical Predication and the Appeal to Symbolic Meaning

We have seen that the class of religious sentences includes sentences which are noncognitive (blessings, prayers, commands, and exhortations), sentences which are cognitive and are to be taken as *literally* true if true at all (historical, descriptive, predictive, explanatory, and autobiographical sentences), and sentences which are set forth as cognitive but which are not to be interpreted literally or treated as *straightforward* empirical hypotheses at all. The latter are to be viewed as analogical sentences and the terms employed in them are to be viewed as having analogical—not literal—meaning.

[18] Robert Leet Patterson, "Universal Religion and Special Revelation," in *The Review of Religion,* vol. 10 (May, 1945), p. 353.

This appeal to analogy is one of the qualifying devices to which Flew makes reference when he speaks of religious claims dying "the death of a thousand qualifications." [19] We will now ask if the doctrine of analogical predication can enable those religious sentences which are set forth as cognitive but nonliteral sentences to retain their cognitivity. This doctrine is not only important historically (with St. Thomas and scholasticism); it also constitutes the means whereby a number of contemporary philosophers and theologians attempt to retain the cognitivity of religious sentences, and hence is deserving of our careful attention.[20] We will first present the doctrine of analogical predication as we find it in its clearest and best argued form. Then we will argue that this doctrine will not perform the function for which it was devised, namely, that of avoiding both univocal and equivocal predication while retaining the cognitivity (factual meaningfulness) of religious sentences.[21]

In his *Existence and Analogy,* E. L. Mascall provides the clearest formulation of the doctrine of analogical predication of which we are acquainted. The analogical relation between God and the world must be viewed, he tells us, as combining in a tightly interlocked union both analogy of attribution and analogy of proportionality. This union, he argues, provides a means whereby the cognitive (though not literal) significance of religious sentences about God can be shown.

In setting forth his doctrine of analogical predication, which unites analogy of attribution and analogy of proportionality, Mascall agrees with Gilson that the purpose of the doctrine of analogy is not to allow us to form concepts of the divine essence, but to allow us to affirm the divine existence; not to compare God's features with those of finite beings, but to allow us to assert that he exists when we can identify him only by describing him in terms

[19] See chapter six.

[20] See, for example, Raphael Demos, "Are Religious Dogmas Cognitive and Meaningful?" part of a symposium with C. J. Ducasse, Eastern Division, American Philosophical Association, published in *Academic Freedom, Logic, and Religion,* Morton White, editor (Philadelphia: University of Pennsylvania Press, 1953).

[21] The schoolmen mean by univocal predication the application of a term to both x and y, the meaning of the term being exactly the same in the two cases. In equivocal predication the term is applied to two objects in two completely different senses of the term.

derived from the finite order. Mascall approvingly quotes one of Gilson's remarks on St. Thomas's treatment of analogy:

> St. Thomas undoubtedly does allow us a certain knowledge of God, and unless we are to admit that St. Thomas has grossly contradicted himself, we must suppose that the knowledge of God which he grants does not in any way bear upon his essence. . . . Every effect of God is analogous to its cause. The concept which we form of this effect can in no case be transformed for us into the concept of God which we lack, but we can attribute to God, by our affirmative judgment, the name that denotes the perfection corresponding to this effect. To proceed in this way is not to posit God as similar to the creature, it is to ground oneself on the certitude that, since every effect resembles its cause, the creature from which we start certainly resembles God.[22]

For Mascall the doctrine of analogy enables us to attribute to God the perfections which correspond to the effects of his created world. It does not enable us to conceive of God's goodness or his anger, for no concept of the essence of God can be formed by a finite mind. The meaning of analogy is to be grasped by recognizing the contingency of existence which arises from the fact that in finite beings essence and existence are really distinct, whereas in God essence and existence are identical. In the statement, for example, that both a given man and God are good, there is not a formal participation of the same characteristic in the different analogates. Rather, God is described as being good because His relation to His goodness is similar to the relation that a good man bears to his goodness. This does not mean that goodness is to be found formally in God. What is meant, Mascall states, is that the analogue under discussion (like goodness) is found formally in each of the analogates but in a mode that is determined by the nature of the analogate itself. Indeed, this is what is meant by the analogy of proportionality. However, the analogy of proportionality (the view that the goodness of finite beings is to finite being as the goodness of God is to God) which is expressed by Mascall in the following formula:

$$\frac{\text{goodness of finite being}}{\text{finite being}} = \frac{\text{goodness of God}}{\text{God}}$$

[22] E. L. Mascall, *Existence and Analogy* (London: Longmans, Green & Co., Ltd., 1949), p. 118.

is "held together by that analogy of attribution which asserts, not merely in the conceptual but in the existential order, that finite being can exist only in dependence on God." [23] That is, the predicate "good" belongs formally and properly to only one of the analogates, namely, finite being, and "relatively and derivatively" to the other, namely, God. What is meant by "relatively and derivatively" is that in any case where the analogates concerned are God and a creature or created thing, the relation upon which the analogy is based is that of creative causality. Thus, if we say that God and a given man are both good, the content of the word "good" is derived from our experience of goodness of creatures, and we are saying no more than that God has goodness in whatever way is necessary to produce goodness in his creatures.[24] The combined use of analogy of attribution and analogy of proportionality does not enable us to have a concept of God's goodness, anger, or other attributes. It simply permits us to affirm that these qualities or perfections, *whatever they are,* are identical with God's existence. The doctrine of analogical predication still leaves all of our assertions about God "grossly inadequate in so far as they apply concepts to him but they are thoroughly adequate in so far as they affirm perfections of him." [25]

The above, I think, is a fair and accurate summary of Mascall's formulation of the doctrine of analogy. However, for several reasons this doctrine of analogical predication will not do the job for which it was devised, namely, that of permitting theological statements to retain cognitive significance, while at the same time avoiding univocal predication. We will suggest several reasons why this is true. These critical remarks will apply not only to Mascall's position but *mutatis mutandis* to others which employ the doctrine of analogical predication.

The doctrine of analogical predication, it is claimed, enables us "to attribute to God . . . the name that denotes the perfection" corresponding to the effects of God's creation, or as Mascall puts it, "All our assertions about God . . . are thoroughly adequate in so far as they affirm perfections of him." But what does it mean to ascribe a perfection to God? We can have no concept of what any

[23] *Ibid.,* p. 120.
[24] *Ibid.,* p. 102.
[25] *Ibid.,* p. 120.

of these perfections could be. Is it enlightening, having no concept of goodness when applied to God, to say that God's goodness is to God as man's goodness is to man? Is it enlightening, having no concept of anger when applied to God, to ascribe anger to God, meaning by this that God's relation to the punishments which he imposes is "similar" to that which an angry man has to the injuries which he inflicts? Does this method enable statements about a transcendent God to have cognitive significance? We think not. Such statements could be enlightening only if we had some literal knowledge of God. That is, if one is to know analogically something of God (or any other object), then one must know something of God (or any other object) *literally*. The assertion, for example, that God's goodness is to God as man's goodness is to man is significant to the extent that we know something nonanalogical about God, namely, something about the meaning of goodness when applied to God. Otherwise the analogy conveys no meaning. In fact, it would appear that some nonanalogical knowledge of God is necessary in order to know that certain analogies are appropriate ones to apply to Him.

This objection can be put in another way. It is a quite meaningful use of analogy to take any given characteristic of our experience and postulate a much higher degree of that characteristic than our experience actually shows. Thus though the meaning is not precise, it nonetheless is quite meaningful to speak of men attaining a much higher degree of moral goodness than they now have. However, the use of analogy in religious utterances requires much more than differences in degree of some characteristic found in our experience. The religious use of analogy requires that the characteristic alluded to in human experience (for example, goodness or knowledge) be fundamentally *different in kind* when offered as an attribute of God. The characteristic does not differ merely in *degree*, for God possesses these characteristics in an absolute or unlimited sense. God is "infinitely good" and "infinitely wise." These religious utterances go completely beyond the use of analogy viewed as a movement to a higher degree of a characteristic found in our experience, for, when these attributes are predicated of God, we are speaking of something unconditioned and unlimited. That God possesses the qualities of infinite goodness and infinite wisdom conveys no meaning, since the difference between human goodness and knowledge and divine goodness and knowledge is not one of *degree* but one of *kind*. These "infinite" qualities do not have the experiential grounding required for meaningful comprehension.

There is a further problem involved in the theologian's use of analogical predication. If something literal about God is not known, then one becomes involved in invoking one analogy in order to explain another analogy. Paul Hayner points out that this is exactly the predicament that St. Thomas is in when he remarks that an effect can be said to *resemble* God solely according to analogy.[26] The notion of resemblance itself must be viewed analogically. We can say, for example, that God's goodness resembles that of man. But it is not only the case that goodness is to be viewed analogically when applied to God; it is also the case that the relation of resemblance must be viewed analogically. This seems to leave one in a regress of analogical explanations. If this is true, then surely the appeal to analogy loses its value as a means whereby the meaning of theological statements can be fixed.

There is a further problem for some theologians who want to rely on analogical predication. The unknowable qualities, like goodness or anger, which are attributed to an unknowable transcendent being cannot be properly spoken of as attributable at all. This is the case because God's nature is viewed as simple and incomposite. God's existence and his ascribed attributes are stated as being identical with his essence. But if there are no relations in God, then the relation of attribution is also ruled out. Or is the relation of attribution itself to be viewed analogically? If so, the theologian is left in the uncomfortable position of attributing unknowable properties to an unknowable being, using an unknowable relation of attribution. The "cloud of unknowing" is a complete overcast.

Our objections to analogical predication can also be stated in the following manner: Predicates, like "goodness," when applied to God have been so "eroded" (to use Antony Flew's notion) of their ordinary meaning that they appear no longer to have meaning at all. We are told that the goodness of God and the goodness of man differ in degree, and it is assumed that this gives theological state-

[26] Paul Hayner, "Analogical Predication," in *Journal of Philosophy*, vol. LV (September 25, 1958), p. 857.

ments an empirical grounding and some sort of cognitive meaning, such that one then knows what is being asserted. However, it is added that this difference in degree between the goodness of God and the goodness of man is *infinite,* whatever that means. The force of this qualification seems to make the statement "God is good" compatible with any possible occurrence, so that no evidence at all could possibly confute it. But if this is the case, can we say that it means anything at all? The application of the predicate "good" (and others) to God will be compatible with God's being of any character whatsoever, and, consequently, nothing whatsoever will follow from the fact that the predicate "good" (and others) applies to God.

For the above reasons, we do not think that the doctrine of analogical predication fulfills the function that Mascall (among others) wishes it to perform, namely, that of giving cognitive meaning to statements about a transcendent being. It does not enable statements about God to conform to the falsifiability test—such that the speaker and hearer know or can find out what the statement is about and the extent of the claim which is being made.

Some current thinkers (W. T. Stace and Paul Tillich) maintain that religious sentences have objective import but that both their meaning and their truth are "symbolic." This appeal to symbolic meaning, it seems to me, is often simply a form of the doctrine of analogical predication. Like the doctrine of analogy, it denies that religious sentences are to be taken literally. The problem, however, lies in specifying the meaning of any given "symbolic" religious sentence. We have already seen the difficulties in discovering some clear meaning for analogical religious sentences. These same difficulties confront the view that the meaning of religious sentences is symbolic.

Without any attempt to treat Professor Tillich's position in detail (a task clearly beyond our scope), and hence with the danger of oversimplification, let us point to these difficulties within Tillich's view of religious language. His thesis is that the content of religious faith is not literally or empirically true but symbolically true. God, for Tillich, is "the unconditioned transcendent," surpassing every conception of *a* being. Speaking of religious symbols, he states:

> They must express an object that by its very nature transcends everything in the world that is split into subjectivity and objectivity. A real

> symbol points to an object which can never become an object. Religious symbols represent the transcendent but do not make the transcendent immanent. They do not make God a part of the empirical world.[27]

In some sense religious symbols "represent the transcendent" and "not merely the subjective character of a religious individual." They have objective reference but not objective empirical reference; nor is their meaning literal. The only literal statement about God is that "God is being-itself"; everything else must be said in symbolic terms.

At least two problems confront Tillich's view. The first concerns the vagueness of the only nonsymbolic statement about God—"God is being-itself." Is "being-itself" or "unconditioned transcendent" a descriptive expression? What does it mean? Tillich himself warns us that its meaning is not to be identified with the concept of existence. Only particular things exist, and God cannot be reduced to a particular. This, however, doesn't help the philosophical analyst concerned with the meaning of this statement, for if "is" or "being" does not assert the particular existence of something, then what does it assert? He knows that "being" or "is" is a word with a variety of logical functions, nonreferring uses or functions. It denotes identity, class inclusion, and predication. But pointing to these functions does not help Tillich. The only clue we have from Tillich is that the meaning of "God is being-itself" is to be had by thinking about what we mean when we say something is. This has led one commentator to ask this question: "Are we to understand that God is what unicorns and the Eiffel Tower have in common?" [28]

Secondly, and perhaps more fundamentally, God, as the ground of all being or as being itself, is "beyond all differentiations that mark off one sort of being from another." [29] God is "'beyond' the split between essence and existence." [30] We can say nothing nonsymbolical about being-itself. This being the case, a given symbol, in

[27] Paul Tillich, "The Religious Symbol," in *Religious Experience and Truth*, edited by Sidney Hook (New York, 1961), p. 303.

[28] J. M. Hinton, reviewing Tillich's *Theology of Culture* in *Mind* (July, 1960), pp. 424-426.

[29] William P. Alston, "Tillich's Conception of a Religious Symbol," in Hook, *op. cit.*, p. 17.

[30] Paul Tillich, "The Meaning and Justification of Religious Symbols," in Hook, *op. cit.*, p. 8.

the words of Alston, "cannot be judged in terms of the reality of that aspect of being itself which it is being used to symbolize. We are unable to specify any such aspect. Symbolic utterance becomes the primary, and indeed the only, type of religious utterance." [31] This really means that there can be no intelligible characterization of "being-itself" or God.

Suppose, for example, that God or "being-itself" were characterized as omniscient. He knows everything. Now it could be argued that this statement is metaphorical or symbolic. The concept "knowledge" is used in speaking of God but used symbolically, for God's knowledge is perfect, far exceeding that of human beings (the normal home of the concept). God's knowledge is of the same kind as that of human beings, but it is of a much higher degree. Thus employed, the concept "omniscient" has an intelligible use when applied to God. It communicates something to us. But note also that it is an anthropomorphic use.

Is this possible use of symbols about God open for Tillich? Clearly not. In the words of Professor Clarke, Tillich

> seems to want to say that the negative element in the assertion "God knows everything" is due to the fact that God *transcends knowing* because he is the ground of knowledge and the affirmative element is due to the fact that God *includes knowing*—but our knowing, not his. This not only fails to tell me precisely what it is that is affirmed and negated in knowledge, it merely expresses these elements symbolically, for "ground," "transcends," and "includes" are all spatial metaphors. If they are not spatial metaphors, they are at least relations, and according to Tillich, "the holiness of God requires that in relation to him we leave behind the totality of finite relations and enter into a relation which, in the categorical sense of the word, is not a relation at all." Thus, relations are not literally applicable to God, since he is the ground of all relations; they, too, "disappear in the ground of being, in being-itself." Is this not again "the night in which all cows are black"? [32]

[31] William P. Alston, *op. cit.*, p. 18.

[32] Bowman L. Clarke, "God and the Symbolic in Tillich," *Anglican Theological Review* (July, 1961), p. 308.

Professor Clarke's own conclusion is that Tillich leaves us with an ineffable God and forces a "retreat to holy silence." Alston reaches a similar conclusion, stating that for Tillich "the affirmations of religious faith are not subject to criticism in terms of the canons applied by science and common sense to statements of fact." They are in fact completely immune from any sort of criticism. Is this not equivalent to maintaining "holy silence"? Any sentence can be said to be symbolically true—including nonsensical sentences—as long as its symbolic meaning is not specified. Since, on Tillich's showing, the so-called symbolic meaning of religious sentences is not made reasonably clear, then we must infer that his appeal to symbolic meaning does not support the thesis that such sentences have cognitive significance.

It is sometimes maintained that one can be aware of the symbolic meaning of these religious sentences only by having religious experience. Tillich, on occasion, seems to maintain this. It is clearly held by Professor W. T. Stace, who maintains that "the symbolic proposition about God does not stand for another proposition—a literal one—about God. It stands for and represents the mystical experience itself." [33] Again, he remarks that "there is in the moment of mystic illumination an utterly irresistible sense or feeling of conviction. This, it is said, is the most powerful, compelling, coercive, overwhelming experience of which the human mind is capable. . . . The soul stands utterly convinced. Convinced of what? Of a proposition? . . . There is nothing of which the soul is convinced except the conviction itself." [34]

No one denies that individuals have experiences often characterized as religious or mystical. The problem is instead twofold: (1) Is the mystical or religious experience to be characterized as knowledge? (2) Are the propositions generated by the mystical or religious experience to be viewed as having extra-subjective reference or objective import? If the proposition uttered is interpreted as an autobiographical reference to the psychological state of the person having the experience, then the utterance involves no problem. If,

[33] W. T. Stace, *Time and Eternity* (Princeton, 1952), p. 65.

[34] *Ibid.*, p. 121.

however, it is claimed that the proposition has objective import, purportedly being a claim about the existence and nature of a being or entity (or "being-itself") external to the speaker, then the nature and extent of the claim must be made clear. This has not been done. In fact, it is admitted by many of those who have these religious experiences that it cannot be done. This being the case, we are left with the conclusion that such utterances have no cognitive meaning, although they may have meaning of some other kind. We turn now to an examination of a number of contemporary analyses of religious discourse.

CHAPTER SIX

The Left-Wing Response

The Challenge

We have seen that positivism, in the manner in which it has survived, has assumed a very mild form. The self-stultifying effects of the old verification principle have been clearly recognized, and I know of no contemporary philosopher who can be identified as a logical positivist. One of the mild forms in which positivism has survived is found in the principle of falsifiability, first clearly formulated, so far as I know, by Karl Popper.[1] Popper speaks of falsifiability as a "criterion of demarcation," a criterion which enables one to demark statements which belong to the domain of empirical science from metaphysical statements, logic, and mathematics. Presented roughly and simply, it states that a statement has empirical content if it is possible to refute it by experience. The statement need not be verified. It must be testable, but "in a negative sense"; some data must be incompatible with it. In fact, "The *empirical content* of a statement increases with its degree of falsifiability: The more a statement forbids the more it says about the world of experience." [2] If a statement forbids nothing, is compatible with everything, it says nothing. It has no empirical content.

Popper is careful to state that his falsifiability criterion is not proposed as a criterion of meaning. "Falsifiability separates two kinds of perfectly meaningful statements: the falsifiable and non-

[1] *The Logic of Scientific Discovery* (New York, 1959); first published in German as *Logik der Forschung* in 1934.

[2] *Ibid.*, p. 119.

falsifiable. It draws a line inside meaningful language, not around it." [3] Popper's criterion, however, *is* a test for empirical meaningfulness. There are other kinds of meaning. These Popper does not want to rule out. But if a statement is not falsifiable, then it has no empirical content.

The influence of Popper's falsifiability criterion is obvious today. This mild form of positivism is in fact adhered to by many contemporary philosophers of religion. Its mildness and lack of dogmatism (it doesn't attempt to kill metaphysics by calling it names) have been attractive to many Christian thinkers, who have attempted to show that this form of positivism and Christianity are compatible. Antony Flew formulates the falsifiability challenge in *New Essays,* and his challenge has elicited a variety of responses. He writes:

> Suppose that we are in doubt as to what someone who gives vent to an utterance is asserting, or suppose that, more radically, we are sceptical as to whether he is really asserting anything at all, one way of trying to understand (or perhaps it will be to expose) his utterance is to attempt to find what he would regard as counting against, or as being incompatible with, its truth.[4]

If nothing is incompatible with the truth of a purported statement, then, Flew claims, the statement asserts nothing. More specifically, he asks the religiously minded: "What would have to occur or to have occurred to constitute for you a disproof of the love of, or the existence of God." [5] Concerning the love of God, suppose that someone

> tells us that God loves us as a father loves his children. We are reassured. But then we see a child dying of inoperable cancer of the throat. His earthly father is driven frantic in his efforts to help, but his Heavenly Father reveals no obvious sign of concern. Some qualification is made —God's love is "not a merely human love" or it is "an inscrutable love"—and we realize that such sufferings are compatible with the truth of the assertion that "God loves us as a father". . . . We are reassured again. But then perhaps we ask: What is this assurance of God's love

[3] *Ibid.,* p. 40; see footnote.
[4] *New Essays,* p. 98.
[5] *Ibid.,* p. 99.

> worth, what is this apparent guarantee really a guarantee against? Just what would have to happen not merely . . . to tempt but also . . . to entitle us to say "God does not love us. . . ." [6]

Flew's point is that the sentence "God loves us" is often made compatible with any possible future experience or series of events, and since it denies nothing, it also does not assert anything. It is the contention of Flew (and of others) that many religious claims "die the death of a thousand qualifications" by being made compatible with any and all data. They are nonfalsifiable and hence have no empirical content.

We will speak of the falsifiability criterion as applied to religion as Flew's challenge. We have noted that many philosophers of religion have responded to Flew's challenge, attempting to make religion compatible with this mild form of positivism. This attempt to reconcile religion with the falsifiability test, however, has led to two fundamentally different analyses of religion and religious language. One group of philosophers responds to Flew's challenge by admitting that "on his grounds he is completely victorious." Religious statements are nonsense even when tested by the falsifiability criterion. They then offer various different "shifting ground" techniques in order to save religion. The various analyses offered by this particular group of contemporary philosophers, though somewhat different, have the general result of leaving religious statements bereft of any cognitive or empirical content. Included within this group are R. M. Hare, J. J. C. Smart, R. F. Holland, Thomas McPherson, R. B. Braithwaite, Ronald Hepburn, and Alasdair MacIntyre. John Passmore speaks of McPherson, one of this group, as occupying the "left-wing of Christian positivism." He applies this term to McPherson because McPherson maintains that the positivist is right—religion is nonsense. This branding of religious assertions as nonsense, McPherson claims, need not be antireligious. It is a "return to the truth about religion." It would not be inappropriate to label this entire group the "left-wing response," for all of them emphasize the nonfalsifiability of religious statements or their lack of empirical content. Nonetheless, all of them in some sense want to retain religion.

[6] *Ibid.*

These philosophers, responding to the falsifiability challenge, tacitly accept the falsifiability principle as a test for factual significance. Their responses, however, are also rooted in their acceptance of the Wittgensteinian account of meaning. They operate, in varying degrees, from within the framework of "conceptual analysis," each emphasizing that we should carefully examine the uses or functions of religious statements or concepts. The falsifiability test is a test for one use or function of language, that of communicating factual or empirical meaning, but language, specifically religious language, has many uses or functions. We find in fact that most of this group argue that the communication of factual meaning is not the primary function of religious discourse. The challenge to which each of these analysts responds is not only to that of Flew but also to the challenge of showing what the logic of religious discourse is.

Another group of philosophers concerned with the meaningfulness of theological statements attempt to meet Flew's challenge head on. They do not attempt to "shift grounds" to save religion or emphasize that the logic of religious discourse is primarily something other than communicating factual information. Nor do they agree that Flew is completely victorious on his grounds. They offer a defense of theological statements as factual assertions, and agree to operate within the falsifiability principle. Included within this group of philosophers are I. M. Crombie, Basil Mitchell, and John Hick. To carry our labeling through, this group may be classified as the "right-wing response."

This chapter and the next may be viewed as a kind of intellectual excursion through the thought of both the right and the left wing. In this chapter we will examine the left wing.

Religion as a Blik: Hare and Hume

One left-wing response to Flew's challenge is R. M. Hare's now famous "blik" theory of religion.[7] Hare maintains that, on the grounds marked out by Flew, Flew has made his case and is victorious. Hare attempts to defend religion by shifting grounds, i.e., by

[7] R. M. Hare, "Theology and Falsification," in *New Essays in Philosophical Theology*, edited by Antony Flew and Alasdair MacIntyre (New York, 1955).

arguing that religious or theological statements are not really *assertions* at all, and hence are neither verifiable nor falsifiable.

Hare tries to make his case—that religion is not a group of assertions about the world but a blik, or attitude, to the world—by relating a parable about a lunatic who is convinced that all dons want to murder him. No matter how many mild and gentle dons he meets, the reply is the same. "Yes, but that was only his diabolical cunning; he's really plotting against me the whole time, like the rest of them. . . ." [8] The undergraduate will accept no state of affairs as counting against his theory about dons. This makes his thesis unfalsifiable and hence his thesis, although it appears to assert something, really asserts nothing at all. It is factually meaningless.

It is important to note, however, that although bliks are not assertions but rather pervasive attitudes toward the world, some bliks, for Hare, are right or sane; others are wrong or insane. All men have bliks, and it is important to have the right ones, and it is clear that Hare holds that the blik of the religious man is the right one. Presumably, we are to view the religious blik as unfalsifiable just as the lunatic's belief that the dons are plotting to murder him, but the lunatic's blik is wrong, whereas the religious man's blik is right.

But what, we might ask, can it mean to say that some bliks are sane or right, others insane and wrong? Surely in the case of the lunatic's blik about dons we say that he is under an obsessional delusion and has the wrong attitude toward dons because he holds his view in the face of any and all evidence concerning the behavior of dons. Those of us who have sane or right bliks about dons do allow the behavior of dons to count for or against our views, and we argue that the evidence does not support the position that dons plot against undergraduates. The claim that the undergraduate is suffering from a delusion about dons is itself grounded on the supposition not only that evidence is relevant to the thesis that dons are plotters but also that the evidence available shows that dons do not plot against undergraduates. But this, of course, would mean that both the sane and the insane bliks about dons are falsifiable and hence were really assertions. It seems to me that Hare's distinction between right and wrong bliks leads to this conclusion, and yet it

[8] *Ibid.*, p. 100.

is clear that this conclusion must be unacceptable to him because he coins the term "blik" specifically to talk about beliefs which are compatible with any and all evidence, beliefs which cannot be refuted. Hare really wants to have it both ways. He wants to speak of bliks as unfalsifiable. But he also wants to speak of sane or right bliks and insane or wrong bliks. If, however, bliks are unfalsifiable, then no state of affairs or evidence can count in comparing different bliks, and this deprives him of the right to distinguish between right and wrong bliks.

Right bliks, then, appear to turn out not to be bliks at all, but falsifiable assertions. His example of the blik about the reliability of steel is subject to the same conclusions which we drew concerning the blik about dons. Hare's attempt to reconcile religion with Flew's analysis by shifting ground and treating religion as a blik fails, for as soon as he brings in the notion of a right blik he reverts to the grounds on which Flew is admittedly victorious.

It may be fairer to Hare, however, if we were to pay more attention to his reference to Hume in connection with his notion of bliks. "It was Hume who taught us," he remarks, "that our whole commerce with the world depends upon our 'blik' about the world; and that differences between 'bliks' about the world cannot be settled by observation of what happens in the world." [9] Bliks, or, in the language of Hume, "natural beliefs," are not themselves factual inferences, but pervasive attitudes toward the world within the framework of which factual inference and explanation take place. For Hume these natural beliefs do not enter into the empirical arena of truth and falsehood. As Hare puts it, ". . . there is no distinction between fact and illusion for a person who does not take up a certain attitude to the world." [10] Those bliks or natural beliefs, for Hume, included belief in the existence of the external world, the identity of the self, and real causal connections in nature. Factual inference or explanation take place within the framework of these natural beliefs.

There is considerable evidence in Hume's works, and I have argued the thesis in some detail elsewhere, that "true" religious

[9] *Ibid.*, p. 101.

[10] R. M. Hare, "Religion and Morals," in *Faith and Logic,* edited by Basil Mitchell (London: George Allen & Unwin, Ltd., 1957), p. 190.

beliefs are treated as natural beliefs by Hume—in the language of Hare, as metaphysical bliks.[11] Hume found in his analysis of knowledge and beliefs that "there is a great difference between such opinions as we form after a calm and profound reflection, and such as we embrace by a kind of instinct or natural impulse, on account of their suitability and conformity to the mind." [12] "True" religion has its foundation in the latter. It is embraced "by a kind of instinct."

When Hume stated in *The Dialogues* that "to know God is to worship Him," he seemed to be saying that religion is the expression of an instinct or an attitude toward the world, and that the proof of such a religious attitude is never the same as that which can be offered to prove a judgment of fact. The former falls properly under natural beliefs, or what Kemp-Smith calls "nonrational synthetic principles which can only be explained as blind, instinctive propensities of the human soul." [13]

Hume's *Treatise* seems to uphold the contention that he classified "true" religious beliefs properly under natural beliefs. In section fourteen, "Of the Idea of Necessary Connection," Hume states that the same difficulties which attend our knowledge of matter and its "unknown forces" also attend our ideas of God. In regard to material objects we can perceive only constant conjunction and cannot reason beyond it. Nonetheless, we do believe in the existence of matter and empirical connections between matters of fact. So also our ideas of the Deity labor under the same imperfections, Hume finds. They are not reasoned ideas; nonetheless, "this can have no effect either on religion or morals," for such beliefs are, Hume seems to say, natural beliefs and "nothing more is requisite to give a foundation to all the articles of religion." [14] Hume further states: "If my philosophy, therefore, makes no addition to the arguments for religion, I have at least the satisfaction to think it takes nothing

[11] See my article, "Hume and Ritschlian Theology," in *The Personalist,* Vol. 42, no. 4 (Autumn, 1961), pp. 561-570.

[12] David Hume, *A Treatise of Human Nature,* ed. by T. H. Green and T. H. Grose, Vol. I (London, 1898), p. 501. (Hereafter referred to as *Treatise.*)

[13] Norman Kemp-Smith, "The Naturalism of Hume," in *Mind,* XIV (1905), p. 156.

[14] *Treatise,* Vol. 1, p. 456.

from them, but that everything remains precisely as before." [15] Hume seems to be saying here that his application of the "experimental method" of reasoning to theological topics neither helps nor hinders religious beliefs, since religious beliefs are not grounded upon any sort of reasoned arguments but upon natural beliefs. They therefore remain the same through all logical or reasoned objections.

Hume's entire philosophy stems from his analysis of the nature of human knowledge. He found a vast difference between the nature of a priori and empirical knowledge, and what he termed natural beliefs, a difference which was consistently neglected and confused in his era. He discovered that when any matter of fact was judged a priori or by rationalistic canons, it could not be proven, since no causes could be established a priori. Here, he maintained, the skeptic could forever be triumphant. The skeptic could also triumph if the religious view of the world were treated as an empirical hypothesis. But there was a sensitive type of belief, not justified by any rationalistic canons or by empirical evidence, which could not be undermined by the skeptic since it was not induced by argument or logical evidence, but rather "flows in upon one with the force of a sensation." Hume was at pains to show that natural beliefs were valid beliefs. By so doing Hume provided, as he states in the *Enquiry,* a basis for the sciences. But in this same distinction he also provided a basis for religious beliefs, which fall likewise under "sensitive beliefs." In fact, Hume distinguishes between two very distinct types of sensitive belief, only one of which is subject to positivistic canons of reasoning. First, there are the sensitive beliefs which are the result of inferences from evidence presented to one in experience. This is the sort of belief Cleanthes has in his argument from design when he asserts that it rests upon the same sort of grounds as the other sciences. To this type of sensitive belief one may apply the canons of reasoning of the "experimental method." But secondly, there is another type of sensitive belief to which the experimental method of reasoning cannot be applied. This "non-positivistic sensitive belief" is the sort that strikes one with the force of a sensation and with such irresistible force that all objec-

[15] *Ibid.*, p. 533.

tions disappear. These nonpositivistic sensitive beliefs, which Hume calls natural beliefs, are never questioned. Though they are not logical, they are the presuppositions on which reason operates, and they are nonetheless to be counted as "realities." The upshot of the *Dialogues* is that theism has firmer grounds under what Hume calls natural belief or under nonpositivistic sensitive beliefs. But keep in mind that Hume insists upon the importance of the distinction between positivistic and nonpositivistic sensitive beliefs. The former, as regards the "theistic hypothesis," ends in skepticism. The latter does not.

Now, if our interpretation of Hume is correct, he was offering the theologian, at least on occasion, the option of shifting grounds (to use Hare's language), of taking religious beliefs out of the empirical circle of truth and falsity and putting them on other grounds, treating them as attitudes toward the world and not falsifiable assertions. As does Hare, Hume enables the religious believer to escape the prongs of the skeptic by putting religious beliefs into the class of nonrational beliefs (*not* irrational beliefs).

But does this procedure of Hume and Hare really enable the religious believer to escape the skeptic? In a sense, yes. Surely, in order for skepticism to enter the picture, there must be something to be skeptical about, i.e., an assertion, a verifiable or falsifiable proposition. And religion ("true" religion, for Hume) does not involve assertions. With the ground thus shifted, the religious skeptic cannot be victorious. But the escape from the skeptic is at the tremendous cost of putting religion completely out of the realm of reason and rational belief, a cost which many theologians will not countenance, for the theologian not only could no longer maintain that his discipline is concerned with fundamental truths about the world, but also he is precluded from distinguishing between right and wrong religious beliefs. To be sure, Hare *does* argue that it makes a great deal of difference to one's life which metaphysical blik one adopts, that there is a great difference in the lives of those who have religious bliks and those who do not, and tremendous differences among those with different religious bliks. This may be true. However, Hare leaves the religious believer in such a position that he is unable to discriminate between right and wrong religious beliefs—much less defend his own.

J. J. C. Smart's Analysis of Religion

J. J. C. Smart attempts to defend religion from Flew's onslaught with a move similar to the shifting ground technique of Hare's blik theory. But the ground to which he shifts is somewhat different. In one essay he indicates agreement with the view of philosophy as logical analysis, as an instrument for avoiding muddled thinking and conceptual confusion.[16] Philosophy "is not the discovery of profound truths about the universe, unattainable by the methods of the special sciences. It is the logical investigation of the concepts of common sense, of science, of history, of ethics, of law, and . . . of religion and theology." [17] Logic or conceptual analysis can enable us to take many metaphysical (for example, the free-will problem) and theological questions, questions which have the appearance of being about the world, and either dissolve them, making them vanish as significant questions, or show that they are really questions answerable within one of the special sciences. It is not clear, however, that all such questions can be dissolved or replaced as factual questions for Smart.

In yet another essay Smart offers rather detailed arguments against the classical arguments for the existence of God.[18] In the course of his treatment of these classical arguments, Smart's own position on theology and his defense of religion come out, i.e., the grounds to which he shifts to prevent Flew from being victorious. He lets us know that he will have no truck with natural theology, and not just because the arguments of the natural theologian are fallacious or inclusive, but because we "believe in the necessity of God's existence because we are Christians; we are not Christians because we believe in the necessity of God's existence." [19] Implicit within this last statement are the grounds of Smart's defense of religion, and specifically the Christian view, against the challenge of

[16] J. J. C. Smart, "Metaphysics, Logic and Theology," in *New Essays in Philosophical Theology*, ed. by Antony Flew and Alasdair MacIntyre (New York, 1955), pp. 12-28.

[17] *Ibid.*, p. 12.

[18] J. J. C. Smart, "The Existence of God," in *Ibid.*

[19] *Ibid.*, p. 40.

Flew. His position becomes clearer with the following remarks: "I draw your attention to the language of religion itself, where we talk of *conversion* not of *proof*. In my opinion, religion can stand on its own two feet, but to found it on a metaphysical argument *a priori* is to found it on absurdity born of ignorance of the logic of our language." [20] If we are aware of the "logic of our language," we see that religion is not a matter of proof or demonstration but rather a matter of attitude and conversion. In fact, the question "Does God exist?" cannot properly arise, not because it is nonsense to assert God's existence, as the positivist claims, but because the "word 'God' gets its meaning from the part it plays in religious speech and literature, and in religious speech and literature the question of existence does not arise." [21] Within the circle of religious converts, the question "Does God exist?" does not arise, and furthermore, for the *un*converted the question has no clear meaning and cannot sensibly be asked. It cannot sensibly be asked for the same reason, Smart claims, that the question "Do electrons exist?" cannot sensibly be asked by the scientifically ignorant. "In order to acquire the concept of an electron we must find out about experiments with cathode ray tubes, the Wilson cloud chamber, about spectra and so on. We then find the concept of the electron a useful one, one which plays a part in a mass of physical theory. When we reach this stage the question 'Do electrons exist?' no longer arises." [22] And before we reach this stage, the question has no clear meaning, for we are too ignorant to know what the existence of electrons involves. The same is true of "Does God exist?" This question does not arise for the converted, and before one reaches the state of conversion the question has no clear meaning. Therefore, in either case the question cannot properly be raised.

Such is Smart's defense of religion. But it is very odd indeed. First, those who are concerned with religion cannot so conveniently be divided into the two camps of the converted and the unconverted. Surely there are some in between, some for whom the question of God's existence is sensible and proper. After all, many believers were previously disbelievers and vice versa, so that even within the

[20] *Ibid.*, pp. 40-41.
[21] *Ibid.*, p. 41.
[22] *Ibid.*

religious perspective the question of God's existence may and does significantly arise. To be sure, the believer generally does not raise the question of God's existence. He takes it for granted. But when a disbeliever or a skeptic calls his attention to the question, he makes every effort to defend an affirmative answer to it. He will not let the skeptic carry the day. His belief in God is firmly grounded in fact, he holds. If Smart is correct, the question of God's existence—the correspondence of one's belief in God to the fact of God's existence—is not a proper or significant question for the believer. This, I think, is simply a false characterization of the believer. In fact, if Smart is correct, then a statement or religious claim such as "The Word was made flesh, and dwelt among us" is reduced to a nonexistential statement describing the beliefs of the Church.[23] Gibson's critique of Smart's view is surely correct: ". . . if the Church believes that the Word was made flesh, as it does, it is not making a statement about its own believing, it is making a statement about the world. It may be right and it may be wrong; but at least it is not merely contemplating its own contemplations." [24] And yet this is exactly the view of theology to which Smart is led by his analysis, namely, that theology is the systematizing of the beliefs of a religious community, with no concern with whether those beliefs correspond to the world. Theology, for Smart, becomes a kind of empirical science, but all that it does is describe and formulate the religious beliefs of a religious community. This apparently is what is left after Smart purges religion of metaphysics. And happily for Smart, this view of theology fits in well with the procedures of logical analysis.

As in the case of Hare's blik theory of religion, Smart's escape from Flew's challenge is at a tremendous cost, the cost in this case being that of depriving the religious believer and theologian of the right to distinguish between beliefs which are simply held by the religious community and beliefs which are true. Since this distinction is precluded by Smart's analysis, he is left in the position of offering protection to any kind of nonsense or superstition which comes along. Smart "saves" religion by making religious beliefs

[23] A. Boyce Gibson, "Modern Philosophers Consider Religion," in *The Australasian Journal of Philosophy,* Vol. 35, no. 3, p. 183.
[24] *Ibid.*

unchallengeable. Passmore's critique of Smart makes our point poignantly: "If one is really prepared to maintain that questions like 'Do ghosts exist?' can never be properly asked except by those who wholeheartedly believe in ghosts, and therefore will not want to ask this question, then no doubt religion is 'saved'—but so is every form of superstition." [25] Smart's conclusion, then, that "it is possible to hold that the question 'Does God exist?' is not a proper question without necessarily also holding that religion and theology are nonsensical" [26] is indeed expensive, far too expensive for many theologians and religious believers.

Many theologians, I am sure, would be quite unhappy with Smart's reduction of theology to the analysis and systematizing of beliefs held by a religious community. They want to insist that their discipline is concerned with fundamental truths—the most fundamental ones—about the world. Smart, however, with his animus against metaphysics and natural theology and his view that there is nothing to investigate beyond the range of the natural sciences, can offer nothing other than this impoverished (many would claim) view of religion.

Religion as "Retreat Into Silence": McPherson

Thomas McPherson evidences concern over the challenge of the positivists and the "worry" over the meaningfulness of theological statements. His unusual response to the challenge is intermarriage, a wedding of positivism and religion. "What to the Jews was a stumbling-block and to the Greeks foolishness is to logical positivists nonsense." [27] But, McPherson goes on to say, there is more to be learned from this than is realized by most theologians. The positivist's position is not only compatible with religion; it can also be of tremendous help to the believer and theologian by ridding them of misconceptions of religion. The basic misconception of

[25] J. A. Passmore, "Christianity and Positivism," in *The Australasian Journal of Philosophy,* Vol. 35, no. 2 (1957), p. 134.

[26] Smart, *op. cit.*

[27] Thomas McPherson, "Religion as the Inexpressible," in Flew and MacIntyre, editors, *New Essays in Philosophical Theology* (New York, 1955), p. 134.

religion is that it is a cognitive enterprise, that religious utterances are capable of being true or false and can be tested for sense and nonsense in the same manner as other ordinary statements. The theologian goes wrong in involving himself in metaphysics or natural theology or in any way treating religion as a cognitive enterprise. "The things that theologians try to say (or some of them) belong to the class of things that just cannot be said. The way out of the worry is retreat into silence." [28] What the positivists have done is to show the absurdity of what theologians try to say, and in effect they have "helped to suggest that religion belongs to the sphere of the unutterable." [29] They are, then, not the enemies of religion, but the enemies of theology. The positivist's branding of religious statements as nonsense need not be interpreted as being antireligious. "It can be interpreted as an attack on those who in the name of religion are perverting religion. It can be interpreted as a return to the truth about religion." [30] That truth is that the essential element in religion is its nonrational side, the part that cannot be said or "conceptualized." Since religion belongs in the sphere of the unutterable, ". . . it is not to be wondered at that in theology there is much nonsense (i.e., many absurdities); this is the natural result of trying to put into words—and to discuss—various kinds of inexpressible 'experiences,' and of trying to say things about God." [31]

In support of his thesis, McPherson appeals to both the account of religion offered by Rudolf Otto and to the Wittgenstein of the last passages of the *Tractatus*. Otto argues in *The Idea of the Holy* that the basic element in religion is the "numinous" experience, which is the feeling of creatureliness and the consciousness of the Numen or the Wholly Other. This essential element in religion cannot be conceptualized adequately. McPherson invites us to compare Otto's notion of an inexpressible numinous feeling with Wittgenstein's remarks: "The feeling of the world as a limited whole is the mystical feeling," and, "Not *how* the world is, is the mystical, but that it is." [32] McPherson states that for Wittgenstein the kind of

[28] *Ibid.*, p. 133.
[29] *Ibid.*, p. 141.
[30] *Ibid.*, p. 139.
[31] *Ibid.*, p. 42.
[32] *Tractatus*, 6.44 and 6.45; quoted by McPherson, *op. cit.*, pp. 137-138.

questions that can be properly asked and answered are *how* questions, questions which fall within the realm of natural science. The question asked by the religious man—"Why is there a world anyway?"—is not an answerable question. The question itself is improper: "For an answer which cannot be expressed the question too cannot be expressed." [33] It follows for Wittgenstein, then, that skepticism about religious matters is senseless. "For doubt can only exist where there is a question; a question only where there is an answer, and this only where something can be said." [34]

Wittgenstein allows that men are puzzled about the very existence of the world, that men feel a riddle not answered by the "how" questions and answers. But this feeling of a riddle vanishes when it is seen that such questions cannot be asked. Here, McPherson asserts, is where Wittgenstein and Otto part company, because, for the former, "To see that in religion we are asking questions that cannot be answered is, in a way, to see the pointlessness of religion. For Otto, to see that in religion we are asking questions that cannot be answered is to see its point. . . ." [35] The question "Why is there a world?" vanishes and loses its sense for Wittgenstein, whereas for Otto it retains its significance but it cannot be answered in words.

Whatever the alternative interpretations of Otto and Wittgenstein (and some would maintain that Otto stresses the import of reason in religion equally with the nonrational element), McPherson takes these two philosophers as bulwarks for his view that religion is not a cognitive enterprise and that the theologian should "retreat into silence." McPherson's response to Flew's challenge of the cognitive significance of religious statements appears, for the most part, to be complete agreement that such statements have no cognitive significance. They are attempts to express the inexpressible. On his own ground, Flew is completely victorious, but his opponent, from McPherson's perspective, is a straw man, a man who takes religion to be a cognitive enterprise and who therefore has a misconception of religion. With the correct interpretation of religion (and McPherson's interpretation of religion amounts to a shifting ground technique similar to Hare's), the positivist is not an enemy

[33] *Ibid.*, 6.5.
[34] *Ibid.*, 6.51.
[35] McPherson, *op. cit.*, p. 139.

but an ally, for the fact is that religion *is* nonsense, in one sense of that term.

What are the costs of McPherson's alignment of religion with positivism and his suggestion that religion retreat into silence? Obviously, such a retreat will preclude one religious believer from talking to another about his beliefs or about God. Since religious organizations exist essentially for this function, McPherson's thesis would involve the obliteration of religious organizations. At least their function would have to be altered to that of providing a place to retreat into silence. One wonders how much of religion would be left.

Perhaps a more important consequence of McPherson's thesis that religion is not a cognitive enterprise is that it precludes the possibility of any defense of any one religious view as opposed to others. All religious positions would be treated as on a par. One could not speak of religious truths, nor of religious superstition, for these concepts presuppose that religious statements have cognitive significance. Anything is let in the door.

These consequences, I submit, would be devastating for religion, and McPherson himself seems to be somewhat wary of this fact late in his essay, for he denies that he wants theology to be "adapted to positivistic requirements" in that "theology does not gain by being reduced to the terms of any school of philosophy." [36] This comment is odd indeed, for he has done just that, namely, adapted theology to positivistic requirements. His second thought on the matter, however, is that the "positivistic way" may exclude too much, for "in throwing out the water of theology we may be also throwing out the baby of 'direct,' 'first-order' religious assertions; and this we may well not want to do." [37] But in denying religion cognitive significance he has in fact thrown out "direct, first-order religious assertions" along with theology. We can no longer speak of assertions in religion, but only of religious feelings, emotions, or attitudes. Somehow McPherson does not come to this conclusion. He holds that there are different kinds of nonsense, that Christian beliefs are nonsensical when tested by the literal standards of the positivist

[36] *Ibid.*, p. 143.
[37] *Ibid.*, p. 142.

but that these beliefs are not nonsensical in another sense of nonsense. Religious beliefs have a deeper meaning (not merely emotive meaning, but also cognitive meaning in a sense other than literal) which is unsayable or inexpressible. This deeper meaning cannot be explicated. Even the doctrine of analogical predication will not help, because this too would involve an attempt to express the inexpressible. There is only the security of retreat into silence.

That this retreat affords much security, to the Christian or anyone else, is indeed questionable. If a so-called belief is unsayable, inexpressible, and incomprehensible, can we say that it is a *belief* at all? Even to speak of accepting a belief on faith presupposes that with at least some clarity the belief can be formulated and made comprehensible; for if one does not know what he is believing on faith, can we say that he is believing anything at all? Furthermore, if an utterance is unsayable and incomprehensible, how can we say that that utterance or belief is a Christian belief as opposed to some other kind? Those specifically interested in a defense of Christianity must answer this question.

The general point that we are making is what Bernard Williams calls "Tertullian's paradox with a converse." Tertullian emphasized that fundamental Christian beliefs are paradoxical and incomprehensible, but that these beliefs are to be accepted because they are absurd and impossible. The converse of Tertullian's paradox is that if a belief is absurd, impossible, or incomprehensible, one cannot know what it is for it to be true. In fact (Williams carries the converse further), on Tertullian grounds, ". . . it is difficult to characterize the difference between belief and unbelief. We can indeed point out that the believer *says* certain things which the unbeliever does not say; but we want not just this, but to know *what* it is that the believer believes and the disbeliever does not believe; but this we cannot properly do. But if we cannot adequately characterize the difference between belief and unbelief, we may not be able to characterize the difference between orthodoxy and heresy; for the difference between persons believing different ineptitudes is as obscure as that between those believing one ineptitude and those not believing it. . . ." [38]

[38] Bernard Williams, "Tertullian's Paradox," in Flew and MacIntyre, *op. cit.*, p. 211.

At this point we might bring Wittgenstein back into the picture, not as a bulwark for religion, as McPherson pictures him, but as a severe critic, though not a skeptic, for this Wittgenstein rules out. Wittgenstein's criticism is at the more fundamental level brought out so clearly by Williams. It amounts simply to stating that sentences which are unutterable and incomprehensible all say the same thing—nothing at all. "Why," as Passmore puts the case, "say that God is three in one, rather than four in one, if 'three' and 'one' do not have any literal sense?" [39]

Even an "occasionalist theory of meaning" (a phrase which Passmore humorously coined to characterize the position of the "Barthian" in Prior's dialogue) is of no help. Barthian is made to maintain that nonsense may be given sense by an act of God's omnipotence: "*Of course* we can only talk nonsense when we try to talk about God—our language is the language of sinful men, and is utterly unfitted for such use. *Of course* the laws of thought, and the laws of grammar, forbid us to confess our faith——we try to speak of God, and it is impossible even to begin. But God, with whom all things are possible, comes to our rescue and takes up our words and our thoughts and makes them carry his meaning and his message to men." [40] The Barthian is here suggesting that expressions which in human language are meaningless, are meaningful in God's language, and that God conveys this meaning to men. But alas, this does not solve the problem. Passmore is correct that ". . . if God uses certain expressions to talk to men, then these expressions must have a meaning in a *human language*—one which human beings can learn to use. Not even God can 'give a meaning' to a meaningless expression without giving it a meaning; we must recognize that the expression has a meaning—is not, then, intrinsically meaningless—before we can ask the question 'Who gave it this meaning?' " [41]

[39] J. A. Passmore, *op cit.*, p. 128.

[40] A. N. Prior, "Can Religion be Discussed?" in Flew and MacIntyre, *op. cit.*, p. 9; quoted by Passmore, *op. cit.*, p. 128.

[41] *Ibid.*, pp. 128-129.

Religion Is Not Theology: R. F. Holland

R. F. Holland's essay "Religious Discourse and Theological Discourse" is a sophisticated extension of the ideas we found in McPherson.[42] Holland attempts to make explicit the distinction between religious discourse and theological discourse, a distinction which is implicit in McPherson. McPherson's attack on theology is on the grounds that *any* talk about God must be nonsense. His distinction between first-order religious assertions and theology is a late second thought, whereas with Holland this distinction is more fundamental. For Holland, theology has nothing to do with religion. Theology is talk "about" God, whereas religion is talk "to" God; Holland characterizes religious discourse "roughly by reference to the prayer and worship of 'the seriously religious person' or 'the believer as such' . . ." [43] Religious discourse includes "high level generalizations of religious expression" such as "God is my creator to Whom everything is owed" and "God is the God of mercy, of Whose forgiveness I stand in need," and these generalizations summarize "the believer's attitude to his existence, . . . focusing it directly into an attitude of worship." [44] Holland is careful to insist, however, that religious statements are "not so much about God as about the believer; or perhaps they are statements about the believer's relationship to God." [45] Any request for a description of the object to which the believer is related signifies a "misunderstanding" and results in theology, which, along with metaphysics, is a "product of confusion." Religion is to be saved by completely separating it from theology.

Theology, Holland argues, is either quasi-aesthetic or quasi-scientific. God is treated either as an object of study or contemplation, or as an object of aesthetic enjoyment—" . . . in each case, though

[42] R. F. Holland, "Religious Discourse and Theological Discourse," in *The Australasian Journal of Philosophy*, Vol. 34, no. 3 (1956).
[43] *Ibid.*, p. 148. [44] *Ibid.*, p. 149. [45] *Ibid.*

in a different way, there is an attempt to utilize God." [46] C. S. Lewis (in his *Beyond Personality*) is cited as an example of a quasi-aesthetic theologian, one who speaks of our communion with God through our aesthetic sense. To quasi-scientific theology "belong all those discussions which are marked by a preoccupation with the *existence* of God and hence by speculation as to when or where God might exist and what sort of an existence God might have." [47] Here there is concern with evidence and proof and a "pretension to the rise of scientific criteria, in spite of the fact that there is no scope at all for the development of techniques of measurement and calculation, no apparatus to build, no predicting, no possibility of arranging an experiment." [48]

Holland insists that "there are many possible objects of study and aesthetic enjoyment, and God is not one of them." [49] Theologians suffer from "conceptual myxomatosis," identifying religion with what it is not. In religious discourse, knowledge of God, Holland asserts, is not "synonymous with the knowledge that God exists and though it might be supposed that it must at least *include* the knowledge that God exists, I think that this supposition must be a misunderstanding. The idea of God's existence may enter into religious discourse when a religious person asserts that God exists as a way of affirming his religious belief, his belief *in* God. But if in making this assertion he takes himself to be saying, not simply *that* he believes in God, but *what* he believes in regard to God (i.e., that God is a being who exists) then I think that he passes at once from religious discourse into theology; he has started to talk *about* God and in a quasi-scientific manner." [50]

Along with his critique of theology, Holland insists upon retaining the distinction between religion and superstition, a distinction "which is of vital importance if religion is to be taken seriously." "Knowledge of God" also is a phrase which has a place in religious discourse, but it is not to include epistemological notions such as evidence, hypothesis, and proof—such as one finds in theol-

[46] *Ibid.*, p. 151.
[47] *Ibid.*, p. 154.
[48] *Ibid.*
[49] *Ibid.*, p. 155.
[50] *Ibid.*, p. 160.

ogy. " 'Blessed are the pure in heart for they shall see God.' This does not mean 'Blessed are the pure in heart for they shall have special experiences with a cognitive content.' " [51] Knowledge of God within religious discourse is "related to the love of God, to the sinner's repentance and his striving to do God's will. . . ." [52] Such knowledge of God cannot be viewed as knowledge *about*. The request for knowledge *about* God is "inappropriate and logically unsatisfiable. . . ." God's existence does not involve some sort of factual hypothesis, and to so treat it is detrimental to religion. Quasi-scientific knowledge of God would in fact "render religious belief superfluous—would involve a positive cessation of faith, since it would replace it by a take-it-or-leave-it acceptance of fact." [53] It is contradictory, Holland claims, to speak of having religious faith in a fact. He denies that there is "even the possibility of a 'cognitive encounter' with the object of faith; which is to say that the object of that faith cannot be any sort of existent." [54] To those who insist that religion, prayer, and worship would lose their sense unless our prayer and worship are directed to someone who exists, Holland replies: "But, I ask, what sense would worship lose? For if it cannot be clear to anyone what the sense of worship is without it being said that God is a being (an existent), then I do not see how it can become clear when this *is* said, since the sense of the assertion that God is a being is itself, to say the least, unclear." [55] To be sure we can say, for Holland, that God exists and that He is the Creator, but "what makes it possible for the assertion that God created the world to have (religious) truth is not that some big cosmological event should have taken place, but that this assertion should be uttered by one who is grateful for his existence and finds it good." [56]

Such is Holland's attempt to save religion by distinguishing religious discourse from theological discourse. Having saved religion, what remains of it? Religious discourse, if it is to include any cognitive component at all, is reduced to autobiographical statements

[51] *Ibid.*, p. 159.
[52] *Ibid.*, p. 160.
[53] *Ibid.*, p. 161.
[54] *Ibid.*
[55] *Ibid.*, p. 162.
[56] *Ibid.*, p. 163.

about the believer. No predicates can be applied to God. In fact, we cannot view God as having any sort of existence. In denying even the possibility of any cognitive encounter with the object of faith, and in ruling out of religious discourse any talk *about* God, Holland relegates religion totally to the realm of the nonrational. All that is left is prayer and worship. Prayer and worship to what? Not to an existent being. Holland speaks of "the object of faith." But what could the object of faith be? Even this question is illegitimate, for it leads to theology. But this means that the object of faith could be anything at all or nothing at all. Holland seems to think that ridding religion of all cognitive components not only does not injure religion but also is necessary to preserve it. Recall his claim that it is self-contradictory to have faith in a fact, an existent thing. Is it not the case, however, that faith, prayer, and worship lose their point unless there are at least some beliefs or statements about God which form a backdrop for these activities? "The end needle point of faith," Williams remarks, is "to pray just to the unknown God, in complete ignorance of whether such an activity had any sense in relation to him or not—or rather, in such ignorance, one would have to say 'it' rather than 'him'; and could one even say that? Something must be believed, if religious activities are not just to be whistling in the dark without even the knowledge that what one is whistling is a tune; and something that connects God with the world of men." [57] Such beliefs, however, would make theology an essential part of religion, and would in fact obliterate Holland's distinction between religious and theological discourse. Holland's position has Barthian overtones, and Gibson appropriately remarks of Holland that "to attach oneself, in 1956, to German theology and British philosophy is to make the worst of both worlds." [58] We are arguing that if religion is to retain its significance in the lives of men then at least some beliefs *about* God, some cognitive content, must remain intact. How could one retain the distinction between religion and superstition, which Holland thinks is essential, unless this were so?

Furthermore, unless Holland is simply setting forth an arbitrary and prescriptive definition of religious discourse, his thesis is surely

[57] Bernard Williams, "Tertullian's Paradox," in *New Essays in Philosophical Theology* (New York, 1955), p. 210.

[58] Boyce Gibson, *op. cit.*, p. 178.

descriptively false. Within religious discourse the request for specification of one's belief, and even for a description of what one takes to be the religious object, is viewed as quite proper. Such questioners are not sent away with the remark: "Your question is logically improper and indicates a misunderstanding of religion."

Again, to question Holland's sharp distinction between religious and theological discourse on other grounds, is it not the case that what he calls religious discourse is itself determined by theological discourse? Cameron cites the example of the fathers of Chalcedon who were faced with those who said that Christ was altogether a creature, those who said that he was not a man, and those who said that the Divine and the human co-exist in him but were not united.[59] Their reply was drawn from what Cameron calls the "philosophical word book" of the period. As concerning his Godhead, Christ was held to be *homaousias* with the Father; the Godhead and the manhood were viewed as united in one *hypostasis;* and Mary, in consequence, was said to be the *Theotokos.*[60] This kind of discourse, which Holland would call purely theological, has in fact determined the character of Christian religious discourse, and this fact should make one suspicious of any attempt to completely separate religion from theology, belief *in* God and talk *to* God in prayer and worship from beliefs *about* God.

A Conative Theory of Religion: Braithwaite and Hepburn

R. B. Braithwaite in his Eddington Memorial Lecture, *An Empiricist's View of the Nature of Religious Belief,* responds to Flew's challenge with another shifting ground technique devised to save religion. He maintains that religious statements are not empirical claims because they are not testable by experience. Nor are they necessary propositions. But we cannot infer from this, as the positivist does, that religious statements are meaningless, for, if such statements "have a use they surely have a meaning—in some

[59] J. M. Cameron, "R. F. Holland on 'Religious Discourse and Theological Discourse,'" in *The Australasian Journal of Philosophy,* Vol. 34, no. 3 (1956), p. 206.

[60] *Ibid.,* p. 207.

sense of meaning." [61] The verification principle is to be made into the "use principle," the Wittgensteinian notion that the meaning of any statement is given by the way it is used. For Braithwaite it follows that "the kernel for an empiricist of the problem of the nature of religious belief is to explain, in empirical terms, how a religious statement is used by a man who asserts it in order to express his religious conviction." [62] Examination of such use, Braithwaite claims, justifies the assimilation of religious to moral assertions. Moral judgments make no factual claims. Nor can they be viewed as mere expressions of emotion. They are expressions of intentions to subscribe to a policy of action. Braithwaite calls this view a *conative* theory of ethics. Religious statements also express commitment to a policy or way of life. ". . . the intention of a Christian to follow a Christian way of life is not only the criterion for the sincerity of his belief in the assertions of Christianity; it is the criterion for the meaningfulness of his assertions. Just as the meaning of a moral assertion is given by its use in expressing the asserter's intention to act, so far as in him lies, in accordance with the moral principle involved, so the meaning of a religious assertion is given by its use in expressing the asserter's intention to follow a specified policy of behavior." [63] The Christian's assertion that God is love Braithwaite interprets to be a declaration of an intention to follow an agapeistic way of life. It is not the predication of a property to an existent being. The whole body of Christian assertions he interprets as intentions to follow an agapeistic life, but he grants that the meaning of religious assertions will be different for different people depending upon the form of behavior to which one feels the religious assertion commits one.

Braithwaite agrees that there are differences between religious and moral statements. Unlike moral statements, the interpreted-behavior policy is not specified by one assertion. Furthermore, religious assertions concern internal as well as external behavior. More fundamentally, a religious assertion has "a propositional element which is lacking in a purely moral assertion, in that it will refer to a story

[61] R. B. Braithwaite, *An Empiricist's View of the Nature of Religious Belief* (Cambridge: Cambridge University Press, 1955), p. 10.

[62] *Ibid.*, p. 11.

[63] *Ibid.*, p. 16.

as well as an intention."[64] A "story" (or an "allegory," "fable," "tale," "myth"—terms which Braithwaite says might also be used) is a "set of propositions which are straightforwardly empirical propositions capable of empirical test (even if they are about mythological beings who never existed but who would have been empirically observable had they existed) and which are thought of by the religious man in connection with his resolution to follow the way of life advocated by his religion."[65] It is not necessary that the stories be believed but only that they have a meaning and be entertained in thought; for the function of such stories is that of assisting one to follow a way of life or policy of action. The import of religious stories is psychological and causal. "It is an empirical psychological fact that many people find it easier to resolve upon and carry through a course of action which is contrary to their natural inclinations if this policy is associated in their minds with certain stories. And in many people the psychological link is not appreciably weakened by the fact that the story associated with the behaviour policy is not believed."[66] Not only is it the case that such stories need not be believed—they need not even be consistent. "Indeed a story may provide better support for a long range policy of action if it contains inconsistencies."[67] This contention further reinforces Braithwaite's thesis that religious stories are not to be viewed as logical justification for a belief, but as psychological support in following a way of life. He concludes that his account of religious belief does justice both to the demand of the empiricist that meaning be tied to empirical use and to the claim of the religious that their beliefs be taken seriously.

Such is Braithwaite's analysis of religion from the viewpoint of the empiricist or one who employs the "use principle." Portions of it certainly have plausibility, and it may be difficult to come up with another theory of religion which is compatible with the principles of empiricism. If this is the case, then many will want to draw the obvious conclusion that traditional religion with its emphasis upon a cognitive component is simply incompatible with such empiricism.

[64] *Ibid.*, p. 24.
[65] *Ibid.*, p. 23.
[66] *Ibid.*, p. 27.
[67] *Ibid.*, p. 28.

Braithwaite in fact is saying just that in offering his solution to the claim that religious statements be taken seriously and that they be meaningful. For what is meant by taking religion seriously and viewing religious statements as meaningful? Just that religious statements, as commitments to a policy of behavior, and religious stories have an important psychological and causal effect upon human beings. Surely no one denies this. But is it not the case that the religious man wants his view taken seriously as a truth claim, as a claim with cognitive meaning, a claim about the nature of the universe as it were? Braithwaite's analysis precludes this possibility. This fact itself is not odd or unusual. What is odd is that Braithwaite seems to think that his account of religious statements is compatible with traditional Christianity. Is it the case that a Christian may disbelieve in the historicity of Jesus Christ and in the existence of God and yet remain a Christian? Is it the case that the Christian need not be committed to certain beliefs *about* the nature of the universe and of man's relationship to it? Surely these questions must be answered negatively. One must do more than commit oneself to a certain way of life and entertain certain stories in order to be a Christian. One must believe something. Braithwaite holds, however, that one need believe nothing. In fact, the only objection to speaking and thinking of Christ or God with complete derision stems from the facts of empirical psychology,[68] namely that such thinking and speaking are not psychologically efficacious in leading one to follow an agapeistic way of life. As I see traditional Christianity, Braithwaite's view is incompatible with it. This, of course, is not a criticism of Braithwaite's view.

Ronald Hepburn, who subscribes to Braithwaite's view with some qualifications, clearly recognizes the incompatibility of this view with traditional Christianity. Nonetheless, he finds it attractive to the "religiously minded sceptic" or to one who wants to combine religion and empiricism. Hepburn simply rejects traditional Christianity and the view of religion as a cognitive enterprise. All that is necessary for a set of attitudes and beliefs to be properly called religious are three conditions. First, the believer must "commit him-

[68] H. J. B. Horsburgh, "Professor Braithwaite and Billy Brown," in *The Australasian Journal of Philosophy*, Vol. 36 (1958), p. 206.

self to a pattern of ethical behavior." Secondly, the parable or myth which expresses the way of life chosen and which inspires the believer to practice it must be "tightly cohering." Thirdly, "the parable and its associated pattern of behaviour legislate not for any fraction of the believer's life, but for every aspect of it. It commands his supreme loyalty and determines his total imaginative vision of nature and man." [69] Within Hepburn's scheme, as with Braithwaite's, one can be religious without believing in God or in the "possibility of speculative philosophy." Such beliefs are not necessary, for one "who cannot make sense of the orthodox Christian claims can still give to his life and thought some kind of religious orientation. . . ." [70] He may call upon the "stories" in any sacred book or even in novels such as Dostoevsky's *The Idiot* or Orwell's *Animal Farm.*

It is clear in the case of both Braithwaite and Hepburn that their empiricism, their response to Flew's falsifiability challenge, leads them to reject truth-claims as a prime element in religion, and to what many would consider a very impoverished view of religion. Ignoring the extremely broad definition of religion which they offer and even the further fact that, at least for Hepburn, one could be a Christian, Hindu, and Buddhist at the same time since one could utilize stories from each of these traditions to inspire one to the same way of life, the primary problem for their conative view of theological language is whether the sacrifice of the cognitive element—the belief *that* element—in religion does not leave the believer bereft of the most essential ingredient in inspiring him to practice a certain way of life. Braithwaite and Hepburn maintain that belief *that* is not necessary; in fact, fictitious stories may be more efficacious. This issue itself is an empirical, psychological one. The evidence at my disposal inclines me to agree with Williams, Ewing, and others that some objective belief is necessary if religion is to survive.

One final point on the position of Braithwaite and Hepburn. Some philosophers would criticize their view on the grounds that it

[69] Ronald Hepburn, *Christianity and Paradox* (London: C. A. Watts & Co., Ltd., 1958), p. 195.
[70] *Ibid.*, p. 204.

is a descriptively false account of religious language. The believer does take his views as being capable of truth or falsity, not merely as intentions to follow a policy of behavior. As Hare, on one occasion, puts it, "moral judgments . . . arise out of the religious belief. They do not constitute it." [71] The distinctive aspect of religious belief is *some kind* of factual belief. Braithwaite and Hepburn, however, are quite aware that believers think they are believing something. The point is that the Braithwaite-Hepburn thesis is not to be taken as a descriptively accurate account of what believers think is going on in religious discourse, but rather a prescriptive thesis, a thesis that theirs is the most intelligible account of theological language compatible with empiricism. In effect they are saying: If you want to be a consistent empiricist, then you should adopt a conative theory of theological language.

Alasdair MacIntyre's Analysis of Religion

Among the left-wingers, we save MacIntyre for last. He, more than any of the others, epitomizes the left-wing response to Flew's challenge. "The theologian," he states, "would do well to abandon any suggestion that his assertions are in any sense connected with the way the world goes, as factual assertions are related to the evidence that is relevant to their verification of falsification." [72] In agreement with McPherson, he notes that, although theologians often behave as if their philosophical allies were metaphysicians and their philosophical enemies positivists, nothing is further from the truth. In fact, the positivist does a great service to theology by showing "the impossibility of what the metaphysician seeks to do" and "in so doing he leaves open the possibility of exhibiting religious belief in its own terms." [73] MacIntyre's long essay is in effect an attempt to do just that—exhibit religious belief in its own terms.

MacIntyre makes it clear that he will not accept the strictures

[71] R. M. Hare, "Religion and Morals," in Basil Mitchell, *op. cit.*, p. 180.

[72] Alasdair MacIntyre, "The Logical Status of Religious Belief," in *Metaphysical Beliefs*, edited by Alasdair MacIntyre (London: Student Christian Movement Press, Ltd., 1957), p. 182.

[73] *Ibid.*, p. 211.

placed on meaningfulness by the verification or falsification principle. Every type of discourse has its own logic. What we must do is examine the logic of religious language. In *partial* agreement with Braithwaite, he points out that religious language is vocative and gerundive. Religious myths (MacIntyre stresses that his use of the word "myth" carries no implication as to truth-value) are concerned with the central situations in human life—birth, death, love, and pain. "Any given myth incorporates an attitude to these themes and to accept a myth is to identify oneself with that attitude and so to make the myth directive of one's behavior. To accept a sufficiently comprehensive myth is to accept a whole way of living." [74] MacIntyre, however, will not accept Braithwaite's *complete* reduction of religious myths to declared moral policies. "In worship we are concerned with praising God, not with describing him. But, of course, in worship some assertions are made about God." [75] The religious believer in his use of myth commits himself to the view that those stories say something about God. The problem is how to characterize such assertions.

In characterizing assertions about God, MacIntyre is concerned with two logically distinct issues: (1) to show the meaningfulness of such assertions, and (2) to show "what kind of justification of religious beliefs would be appropriate to their logical status." In order to accomplish this task he purports (which he takes to be the proper task of the philosopher of religion) "only to describe how religious language is in fact used." [76] Such description, he presumes, illuminates both the meaning and the grounds of justification of religious beliefs. MacIntyre gives very little attention to the first issue, and a great deal to the second. Let us examine his remarks on the second issue.

The first point which MacIntyre makes is that religious beliefs are not explanatory hypotheses. If they were, there could be "no justification whatever for continuing to hold them." [77] The attempts of Aquinas, Paley, and Tennant fail, for all the reasons pointed out by Hume. To the extent that theism is set forth as a hypothesis, it

[74] *Ibid.*, p. 191.
[75] *Ibid.*, p. 189.
[76] *Ibid.*, p. 185.
[77] *Ibid.*, p. 196.

is "either false or fantastic. . . ." [78] MacIntyre recognizes the double-edged challenge of the verificationists: interpret religious claims as factual hypotheses, and they turn out to be false; not so interpreted, they are factually meaningless. Referring specifically to Crombie's theory of eschatological verification as one attempt to treat religion as an hypothesis, MacIntyre remarks: "For it does not matter how much more of the picture there is to see." [79] Viewed as a factual hypothesis, the existence of a loving God is incompatible with the needless suffering that exists *now,* no matter what the future holds (a point made so clearly by Paul Edwards[80]). MacIntyre insists that religious beliefs are not hypotheses at all, and to treat them as such is "to falsify both the kind of belief they are and the way in which they are characteristically held." [81] Provisional and tentative adherence is "completely uncharacteristic of religious belief. A God who could be believed in this way would not be the God of Christian theism. For part of the content of Christian belief is that decisive adherence has to be given to God." [82] The essence of Christian belief is "decisive adherence" and "a free decision made in faith and love." Because of this "it is logically inappropriate to give reasons for a religious belief," [83] and "to ask for reasons for or a justification of religious belief is not to have understood what religious belief is." [84] In fact, if proof or demonstration of religion could be provided, religion would be destroyed. "For all possibility of free choice would have been done away. Any objective justification of belief would have the same effect. . . . faith . . . would have been eliminated." [85]

How then are religious beliefs to be justified? MacIntyre's answer is that they are justified by reference to authority. Christians, for example, accept the authority of Jesus Christ. ". . . our grounds for accepting what he says is what the apostles say about him; our grounds for accepting the apostles? Here the argument ends or

[78] *Ibid.,* p. 182.
[79] *Ibid.*
[80] "Some Notes on Anthropomorphic Theology," in *Religious Experience and Truth,* edited by Sidney Hook (New York, 1961).
[81] *Op. cit.,* p. 196.
[82] *Ibid.,* p. 181.
[83] *Ibid.,* p. 209.
[84] *Ibid.,* p. 208.
[85] *Ibid.,* p. 209.

becomes circular; we either find an ultimate criterion of religious authority, or we refer to the content of what authority says." [86] Each religion has its own authority, and one simply accepts a given authority or rejects it. Admittedly, this is the logical correlative of Barthianism in theology, and this means "that religion as a whole lacks any justification." [87] MacIntyre hastens to add, however, that this does not reflect on the logical standing of religious beliefs, for "every field is defined by reference to certain ultimate criteria." [88]

MacIntyre here is making a point concerning the meaning of "justify." That point is that "every chain of reasons must have an ending" and in religion that "end" or "ultimate criterion" is some authority, and to ask for a justification of that authority is "to ask for a something more ultimate than a fundamental conviction. If religious belief were not fundamental, it would not be religion." [89]

Since, then, religious beliefs are justified by reference to authority, since belief in God is not so much believing *that* as "being engrossed by a passion," and since the essence of religion is a free decision made in faith and love, "we ought not . . . to be surprised that to accept religious belief is a matter not of argument but of conversion." [90] The movement from unbelief to belief is not one involving a "logical transition" or "objective considerations," but is "in the person who comes to believe." If someone asks for a justification of a religious belief, all that can be done is to describe the contents of a particular theology or a framework of authority and then wait for conversion.

Such is MacIntyre's description and defense (and it seems that "to defend" for him is nothing other than "to describe") of religion. Several points must be made concerning it. First, MacIntyre explicitly agrees with the verificationist's analysis of religion, namely, that religious beliefs are unfalsifiable even in principle. The *truly* religious person can never allow anything to count against his beliefs. This includes historical evidence, for he explicitly says that "everything of importance to religious faith is outside the reach of

[86] *Ibid.*, p. 200.
[87] *Ibid.*, p. 202.
[88] *Ibid.*
[89] *Ibid.*, p. 209.
[90] *Ibid.*

historical investigation." [91] Although the belief in the Resurrection is a belief about history, the "belief in the Resurrection does not rest on historical grounds. . . . To believe in the Resurrection is to believe more than that Jesus walked out of the Tomb, but it is to believe at least this." [92] The belief is grounded in authority, not historical data.

This thesis is indeed paradoxical, for clearly some religious beliefs are about history, and theologians have been at pains to cite historical evidence in favor of religious beliefs. MacIntyre will grant that religious beliefs include references to historical occurrences, but he will not allow that references to such occurrences have any *logical bearing* on those beliefs. Such occurrences cannot be considered as evidence, for "to the references to an act of God historical inquiry is irrelevant." [93] Surely, however, Mitchell is correct, that if "the occurrence of certain historical events is a necessary condition of there having been a certain act of God (as the empty Tomb of the Resurrection) then historical investigation is certainly *relevant* to the question of the historical event." [94] This is true, even if the religious belief involves more than the assertion of an historical occurrence. This fact is manifest in the attitude of religious believers, many of whom assert that if they could not believe the historical authenticity of the Gospel narrative, they would lose their faith. MacIntyre could respond by claiming that such individuals are not *truly* religious. But surely in this case he would be prescribing what religion ought to be, not describing what religion is. One gets the feeling that MacIntyre, in his essay, is doing more than merely analyzing and describing.

MacIntyre is led to the conclusion that religious beliefs are unfalsifiable and that it is logically improper to cite evidence in their behalf because he conceives of religion as involving unconditional belief and a free choice. To cite evidence is to treat religion as a hypothesis, not as unconditional adherence. Again, one wonders if MacIntyre, in speaking of religious belief as unconditional, is describing or prescribing. At least some religious believers seem to hold their beliefs as hypotheses. Specifically, some Christians attempt

[91] *Ibid.*, p. 206.
[92] *Ibid.*, p. 207.
[93] *Ibid.*
[94] *Ibid.*, p. 215.

to cite evidence of various kinds and not merely appeal to authority. But more importantly, can we not distinguish between the logical status of beliefs and their psychological status (the attitude of individuals toward them). From the point of view of psychological status, religious beliefs might be unconditional. An individual might be living and guiding his life according to such beliefs, and as such he may never question these beliefs or treat them as hypotheses. At the same time, however, the logical status of those beliefs might be provisional. Evidence might be relevant to their truth or falsity.

If this distinction is acceptable, one might agree with MacIntyre that religious beliefs are unconditional, and yet reject his conclusion that it is logically inappropriate to cite justifying reasons for those beliefs. MacIntyre, I fear, will not accept this distinction. But is it not the case that his analysis, in which the notion of unconditional belief means that one must refuse, in advance of all evidence, to reject a belief, makes nonsense of the notion of "belief"? As Mitchell puts it:

> Where a man believes that p, it is a logical possibility to know that p or to doubt whether p; and all these "propositional attitudes" presuppose that there are or could be considerations which justify them. There would be something very odd indeed about a man's saying "I believe that p" and then denying that he had, or needed, any reasons at all for his belief. I am not sure whether we should regard his attitude as intelligible, but irrational, or simply as unintelligible; I think the latter.[95]

MacIntyre's analysis does, of course, permit the giving of reasons in the sense of saying "Read the Bible," or in the sense of describing a theology or authority. But this is not to cite evidence, but only to refer one to authority. In fact, MacIntyre's use of the notion of belief leads us back to the fundamental problem posed by the falsifiability challenge: Do religious beliefs assert anything? MacIntyre himself recognizes that the appeal to authority is of no help here. ". . . if someone asserts 'Twas brillig and the slithy toves did gyre' and when asked what this means replies that it must be accepted on authority, none of our difficulties have been removed." [96]

[95] Basil Mitchell, "The Justification of Religious Belief," in *Philosophical Quarterly*, Vol. 11, no. 44 (July, 1961), p. 219.
[96] *Op. cit.*, p. 199.

This is precisely the problem in MacIntyre's position. His analysis does not remove any of the difficulties concerning the *factual meaningfulness* of religious beliefs. Even presuming that MacIntyre is correct in his account of the justification of religious beliefs (the logical inappropriateness of citing evidence, the appeal to authority, etc.) this is of no help in showing that such beliefs have factual content. He agrees with the positivist that religious beliefs are unfalsifiable but hides in the now popular claim that every type of discourse has its own logic, what Braithwaite calls the "use-principle." Recall, however, that although Braithwaite maintains that religious discourse is meaningful because it has a *use,* he denies that it has factual content. It does not have a semantical use. MacIntyre clearly wants to maintain that religious beliefs have factual content. We worship God but we also talk about Him. However, other than his *description* of religious beliefs and their grounds (which we saw might be *prescriptive*) MacIntyre does nothing to show that religious beliefs are assertions.

We have seen that MacIntyre maintains that religious belief as a "free decision made in faith and love" is incompatible with treating religion as a hypothesis or citing reasons for one's belief. Now, such free decision might be precluded in some sense if a thesis were *completely demonstrable,* although even here one may want to distinguish between the logical status of a belief as demonstrable and the attitude of persons toward it. But surely one can speak of deciding to accept a belief which has evidence in its favor but which isn't conclusively demonstrable. I fail to see any incompatibility in freely accepting such a belief and at the same time offering reasons for it. In fact, as Professor Root puts it, "We could scarcely use the word 'decision' at all if we were acting in the complete absence of any reasons. We might even want to say that we are only truly free to decide when we have fully understood the implications of rational argument on all sides." [97] The notion of freely accepting a belief which lacks any rational grounds is odd indeed, and Root finds in such a notion an "echo of popular existentialism," in which we are condemned to be free but in which all our choices are absurd.

In fairness to MacIntyre, however, it should be noted that his view

[97] Howard Root, "Metaphysics and Religious Beliefs," in *Prospect for Metaphysics,* edited by Ian T. Ramsey (New York: Philosophical Library, Inc., 1961), p. 76.

of the inevitable absurdity of our belief-choices, if we may so characterize it, is tied to his analysis of the limits of reasoning. Every chain of reasons, he tells us, ends somewhere, and where it ends we have "ultimate criteria," some authority for which we opt. If we are able to offer further reasons, then this simply indicates that we have not as yet reached ultimate criteria. Specifically in regard to MacIntyre's appeal to the authority of Christ as ultimate criteria, Mitchell suggests that we enlarge the circle a bit by including the content of what authority says. To the extent that this is done, rational argument (citing evidence) may be extended. ". . . you may find yourself attaching significance to the life and teaching of Christ as the expression of his divinity, to the reanimation of the apostles as evidence of the Resurrection, to the lives of the saints as manifesting the Holy Spirit." [98] Mitchell approvingly quotes Farrar on the importance of reason in religion: "We should not find revelation intrinsically convincing, if everything else made nonsense of it, and it made nonsense of everything else." [99] His emphasis here is upon cumulative evidence of different kinds as *grounds* for faith.

MacIntyre, of course, could grant Mitchell's point (the circle can be extended) and yet insist that somewhere along the line there is an ultimate appeal and an end to reasoning. This issue is of such importance that we will treat it in some detail in chapter eight, where we will be specifically concerned with whether religious claims can be said to constitute knowledge.

We conclude our analysis of the left-wing response with these summary remarks. Although there are significant differences in the positions of the philosophers we have classified under the left-wing response and hence some injustice in applying this label, nonetheless, all of them are similar in certain fundamental respects: (1) They all leave religious claims bereft of empirical content; (2) They make religion out to be essentially nonrational, precluding the possibility of (perhaps even making nonsense of) religious apologetic, insofar as apologetic takes the form of rational argument, and, of course, precluding the possibility of any rational grounds for choosing between religious beliefs.

[98] Mitchell, *op. cit.*, p. 222.

[99] Austin Farrar, "Revelation," in *Faith and Logic*, edited by Basil Mitchell (London, 1957), p. 102; quoted by Mitchell, *op. cit.*

CHAPTER SEVEN

The Right-Wing Response

We turn now to an examination of the positions of those philosophers who attempt to meet Flew's challenge head on—Basil Mitchell,[1] John Hick,[2] and I. M. Crombie.[3] These philosophers accept the falsifiability principle as a test of whether any given claim has empirical content, and they argue that religious claims do conform to their test. For them, religious claims are falsifiable in principle. These philosophers, unlike those we classified under the left-wing response, do not attempt to shift grounds away from the falsifiability test in order to save religion. Flew, in his assault on religion, they claim, is not by any means "completely victorious on his own grounds." On the contrary, religion can be adequately defended even on Flew's grounds. We will call the response of these philosophers to Flew's challenge the right-wing response. We will analyze Basil Mitchell's right-wing response first.

The Response of Basil Mitchell

Mitchell argues that theological claims are factual assertions, and that there is "something odd" about Flew's conduct of the theologian's case. Flew specifically claims that the statement "God loves us" is unfalsifiable. Mitchell simply denies Flew's thesis that

[1] "Theology and Falsification," in *New Essays*; and "The Grace of God," in *Faith and Logic,* edited by Basil Mitchell (London, 1957).

[2] "Theology and Falsification," in *New Essays*; and "The Possibility of Theological Statements," in *Faith and Logic* (London, 1957).

[3] *Faith and Knowledge* (Ithaca, New York), 1957.

the theologian does not allow anything to count against religious assertions. "The theologian surely would not deny that the fact of pain counts against the assertion that God loves men." [4] The problem of evil is generated by exactly such falsifying data. To be sure, the Christian will not allow such data to count decisively against his belief that God loves man. For "he is committed by his faith to trust in God." [5] He will permit states of affairs to count against his belief, but he will never permit his belief to be decisively falsified. His religious beliefs are not, in the words of Mitchell, "conclusively falsifiable," for they are "significant articles of faith." But they are falsifiable.

In order to support his case, Mitchell relates a parable about a resistance fighter who, having met a Stranger, is completely convinced that the Stranger is on his side. Such is his faith in the Stranger that later behavior of the Stranger does not alter his belief. Even when he sees the Stranger turn over his compatriots to the occupying power, the resistance fighter still says: "He is on our side." "The partisan . . . does not allow anything to count decisively against the proposition 'The Stranger is on our side.' This is because he has committed himself to trust the Stranger. But he, of course, recognizes that the Stranger's ambiguous behaviour *does* count against what he believes about him." [6] The resistance fighter's claims, then, Mitchell argues, are falsifiable but not decisively falsifiable. This is also the case in regard to the religious statement that God loves man. The religious man allows that certain data count against his belief, but no data count decisively against his belief.

The plausibility of Mitchell's defense of the falsifiable status of religious beliefs rests upon his distinction between counting against and counting *decisively* against. This distinction, however, may create what Duff-Forbes calls a "verbal illusion, the illusion that the question to whether or not God loves men is an open question, that states of affairs and observable situations are relevant to the determination of its truth or falsity, that states of affairs count." [7]

[4] *New Essays,* p. 103.
[5] *Ibid.*
[6] *Ibid.,* p. 104.
[7] D. R. Duff-Forbes, "Theology and Falsification Again," in *The Australasian Journal of Philosophy,* Vol. 39, no. 2 (1961), p. 149.

Consider the following dialogue. A remarks: "God loves us." B replies: "But look at the needless suffering." A replies: "Yes, that fact counts against my belief, but not decisively." B replies: "You mean that the data concerning needless suffering aren't adequate to overturn your belief? Suppose I offered more evidence of a similar kind. Would it be possible for it to overturn your belief?" A, on Mitchell's showing, is forced to say: "No. No matter how much evidence you cite, it can never be adequate or sufficient to overturn my belief. My faith precludes such an occurrence."

What has happened in the course of this conversation? It seems plain that A has given something with his left hand and has taken it back with his right. His original admission that needless suffering counted against his belief in God's love really amounts to no admission at all as soon as he adds that no amount of data will ever be sufficient to overturn his belief. Mitchell, then, when he says that some evidence counts against but does not count decisively against the belief that God loves men, really means that some evidence *appears* to count against the belief that God loves us *but in fact* no evidence really does count.[8]

Duff-Forbes puts the case in this way: "If the religious man concedes that such-and-such a state of affairs counts against his claim that God loves men, but, because the statement 'God loves men' is an article of faith, allows that it counts against only in the sense that it appears to count against (but really doesn't), isn't it perfectly obvious that states of affairs and observable situations are irrelevant, that they never *do* count *in the required sense?*" [9]

We are led to the conclusion that Mitchell pays lip service only to the falsifiability requirement, that in the last analysis religious beliefs for him are not dissimilar to Hare's religious bliks. In effect, although Mitchell set out to meet Flew's challenge head on, he doesn't meet it at all. He sidesteps, as does a slippery halfback. Unlike the sidestep of a halfback, however, Mitchell's sidestep takes him completely off the playing field. At least, he is not playing Flew's game.

[8] *Ibid.*

[9] *Ibid.*, pp. 149-150.

In another essay Mitchell again concerns himself with the falsifiability demand. He asks what is the empirical basis for the theological doctrine of the grace of God. ". . . if we say that it was by God's grace that St. Paul laboured more abundantly, we seem to be offering a kind of causal explanation, and in that case we ought to be able to defend our explanation by contrasting St. Paul's case with others in which God's grace was known *not* to be at work." [10] Mitchell is concerned over the fact that Christian apologists cannot and will not do this, and he attempts to show that the grace doctrine is experientially grounded, that it is a genuine assertion. It is "not open to scientific test," but it is "not without factual content . . ." [11]

The evidence cited by Mitchell is "the religious experience of individuals and communities," especially the existence of saints, whose strength and graciousness is "somehow incommensurate with what we know of their natural antecedents." Mitchell insists that religious experience, in order to be validating, must be "genuine." Genuine religious experience is the factual ground for the doctrine of grace. How do we test for genuineness? Mitchell's answer is that we must appeal to "a religious tradition to provide us with such an apparatus. . . ." The religious experience of individuals or communities as evidence for God's grace is "not entirely independent, for that experience is interpreted in terms of a religious tradition, based in its turn on the inspired scriptures." [12] For example, the existence of saintliness, the living of a certain kind of life, is cited as evidence for grace. What are the criteria for such a good and virtuous life? Mitchell's answer is that the criteria are found in the Christian tradition. He admits that this appeal is question-begging and circular, for "it is just the criteria of goodness that are often in dispute." [13] St. Paul's list of virtues does not jibe with Aristotle's. In attempting to justify the doctrine of grace, then, reference is made to other more fundamental beliefs in the religious tradition. In the last analysis, the grace doctrine "follows from belief in God" and cannot be substantiated independently of that

[10] "The Grace of God," in *Faith and Logic,* edited by Basil Mitchell (London, 1957), p. 153.
[11] *Ibid.,* p. 161.
[12] *Ibid.*
[13] *Ibid.,* p. 165.

belief, or, for that matter, of an entire religious tradition (including a certain set of values).

Mitchell remarks that, although this procedure looks like complete question-begging and circular reasoning, it is not viciously circular. It seems to me, however, that the procedure *is* viciously circular *unless* somewhere along the line, as appeal is made from one belief to another in the religious tradition in support of grace, at least one of these beliefs is shown to conform to the falsifiability criterion. So far as I can see, Mitchell does not do this, and hence he fails to show that the doctrine of grace conforms to the falsifiability test and has empirical content. This fact is made clearer by one of Mitchell's own concluding remarks. He states, "Belief in the grace of God cannot be established by empirical evidence but once accepted, it can be seen to have empirical application." [14] This statement makes it clear that Mitchell has not really faced the falsifiability challenge, for the question of *what* one has accepted once one has accepted the doctrine of grace is just the problem for the one who offers the challenge. If one accepts the doctrine and can delineate what he has accepted, the request for empirical application is no longer needed.

We are led to the conclusion that Mitchell fails in his defense of the assertion status of religious beliefs. He fails to show that such beliefs conform to the falsifiability requirement.

We turn now to the right-wing response of John Hick.

The Response of John Hick

Hick argues that religious beliefs are falsifiable in principle. To be sure, "the logic of theism is unique and complex," for theism is not an experimental issue. Theism is what Hick calls a "total interpretation" (Hick cites theism and naturalism as alternative total interpretations), and "total interpretations" are neither experimentally testable nor can they be said to be in any degree probable. "Nothing can be said to be probable per se but only in relation to data beyond itself. And in the special case of our experience as a

[14] *Ibid.*, p. 174.

whole there is nothing beyond itself which could stand in a probabilifying relation to it." [15] There is only one universe, and all we can do is offer an interpretation of it on the basis of our experience of it. No such total interpretation can be viewed as being objectively ascertainable. Having pointed to these peculiarities of the logic of faith (which were stated by Hume in different language), Hick offers his own formulation of the falsifiability challenge:

> Would then *any* conceivable happening compel the faithful to renounce their religious belief? There may well of course be psychological limits to the persistence of challenged and discouraged faith, limits which will differ in each individual. But is there any *logical terminus,* any definite quantum of unfavorable evidence in face of which it would be demonstrably irrational to maintain theistic belief? It does not appear that there is or could be any such agreed limit. It seems, on the contrary, that theism is to this extent compatible with whatever may occur. But if this is so, we must ask: Does theism constitute a genuine assertion? [16]

Hick's response to this challenge is that religious beliefs, though not open to refutation, are open to confirmation and hence are genuine assertions. "There can be conclusive evidence for it (religion) if it be true, but there cannot be conclusive evidence against it if it be untrue. For if we survive bodily death we shall (presumably) know that we have survived it, but if we do not survive death we shall not know that we have not survived it." [17] The religious position, then, is cognitively meaningful because it is falsifiable in principle, even if it is never falsifiable in practice. (Should it be false, we could never know it.) The eschatological prediction of the religious view assures its cognitively meaningful status. If the alleged future experience of heaven (Kingdom of God and the Beatific Vision) does finally accrue, then religious theism is verified. Meanwhile, since we are short of heaven, such *possible* experience assures the cognitive meaningfulness of the theistic claim.

Hick, then, uses the device of eschatological verification in order to justify the assertion-status of religious beliefs. But clearly certain

[15] *Ibid.*, p. 135.
[16] *Ibid.*, p. 148.
[17] *Ibid.*, p. 150.

fundamental objections confront this appeal. First, Hick assumes the assertion-status of several religious beliefs (belief in immortality, the Kingdom of God, and the Beatific Vision) in the process of arguing for the assertion-status of other religious beliefs (the belief that God loves us, for example). This is obviously a question-begging technique, for the assertion-status, or factual meaningfulness, of all of these religious claims is under question by the philosophical analyst. There is no objection to Hick's insistence that verification or falsification *in principle,* not verification or falsification *in practice,* is required to guarantee factual meaningfulness. But this doesn't solve his problems, for the same objection confronts those religious propositions the factual meaningfulness of which he presupposes in his defense of the assertion-status of theism. Hick's specific claim is that the believer can conceive of possible experiences which would confirm (experience of Kingdom of God) or refute (experience of an "all-powerful and wholly evil being whose existence precluded the possibility that a God should exist as described by Christianity"[18]) his beliefs. These possible experiences assure the falsifiability in principle of religious beliefs and hence their cognitive status. But surely there is as much problem with the notion of an all-powerful and wholly evil being and the notion of the Kingdom of Heaven as there is with that of an all-powerful, wholly good, loving, heavenly father. It is of no help at all to invoke the former in order to justify the cognitive status of the latter.

Ignoring the question-begging for the moment, however, let us look at another problem in Hick's analysis. The religious believer, he claims, can delineate the meaning of his beliefs now (hence they are falsifiable) because certain possible and conceivable experiences in a postmortem life can be viewed as verifying or falsifying data. However, other parts of Hick's position seem to be inconsistent with this assumption that man can conceive of these possible verifying or falsifying experiences. I have in mind his remark that "whilst the nature or quality of the divine attitudes toward mankind can intelligibly be said to have been exhibited in a human life, their unlimitedness cannot have been similarly disclosed. Jesus, as a human being, was not unlimited in power or knowledge or any

[18] *Ibid.,* p. 156.

other attribute. Infinite characteristics cannot, as such, be incarnated. Nor can they be objects of religious experience."[19] The problem confronting Hick is to explain what is meant by the claim that the nature or quality of the divine attributes can be said to have been intelligibly exhibited in a human life when placed in conjunction with the further claim that none of God's infinite characteristics can be said to have been incarnated or can be objects of religious experience. When we say that God loves us, we cannot understand "love" to mean the *same* thing as the "love" which is exhibited in the life of Christ. For Christ's life "is believed to have been an authentic, but at the same time a finite and limited embodiment of the divine attitude toward mankind. Accordingly when we speak of God discarnate, or God in his transcendent being, we have to put together the incarnated moral characteristics and the 'metaphysical' conception of unlimited being."[20] We can have no knowledge of God as unlimited being. We can have knowledge only of the finite characteristics of Christ, characteristics which are "limited embodiments" of the divine attributes. The problem is discovering the meaning of "limited embodiment of the divine attributes." Will the doctrine of analogical predication help to show how the divine attributes have been intelligibly exhibited or how they can be viewed as limited embodiments of the divine? Can we say that love as exemplified in the life of Christ is *analogous* to the divine attribute of love? Apparently not. For Hick states that the use of analogy is "a negative and formal rather than a positive and substantial answer, for analogous means essentially neither univocal nor equivocal."[21] Since analogous predication will not help, are there other grounds on which we can say that the nature of the divine attributes has been intelligibly exhibited? The appeal to direct religious experience will not help, for Hick denies that infinite characteristics can be the objects of religious experience. Even possible postmortem religious experience cannot be experience of God's infinite characteristics, so that Hick's appeal to eschatological

[19] "Meaning and Truth in Theology," in *Religious Experience and Truth*, edited by Sidney Hook (New York, 1961), p. 206.
[20] *Ibid.*
[21] *Ibid.*, p. 205.

verification is of no help in gaining knowledge of God as infinite being.

It seems clear, then, that Hick's appeal to eschatological verification will simply not do the job for which it was devised, namely, that of assuring the cognitive status of religious claims about God by showing that such claims conform to the falsifiability requirement. Although Hick attempts to fit religion within the falsifiability requirement, he fails for two reasons: (1) He begs the question by presupposing the empirical meaningfulness of some religious claims in the process of proving the empirical meaningfulness of other religious claims; (2) Eschatological verification is of no help in connection with God as infinite being. Yet it is just such religious language, language in which predicates are applied to God as infinite being, which most perplexes those who are concerned with the empirical content of religious statements.

We turn now to I. M. Crombie's defense of the empirical status of religious beliefs. Crombie is quite sensitive both to the demands of the religious believer and to the demands of the philosophical analyst who is perplexed by religious language, and he attempts in his analysis to meet both demands. There are, however, certain fundamental problems confronting Crombie's defense of the empirical status of religious beliefs, and these we will attempt to make clear.

The Response of I. M. Crombie

Crombie agrees that theological statements have the paradoxical features that are generally attributed to them by philosophical analysts. One of these features is that theological statements are to be interpreted as if their subject were a particular individual, and yet they differ in logical character from other statements about individual things. The statement "God is infinite" seems to be very much like "John is tall." Both seem to use a proper name to designate an individual. However, that these statements have different characters is evident from the sort of answers that can be given the questions "Who is John?" and "Who is God?" One can point to John but not to God. "God" resembles a proper name like "John," but differs from ordinary proper names in that its use is not based on acquaintance with the being it denotes. The problem is to discover what sort of meaning can one give the notion of "God" if it is used as a proper name for an individual but violates the criteria of individuality.

The second paradoxical aspect of theological statements is that their predicates employ everyday words but not in everyday senses. Statements like "God loves us" or "God created the world" are at least grammatically like "Mary loves me" and "John built a table." However, the predicates of theological statements are used in such a manner that no factual evidence is permitted to falsify them. Ordinary statements are delimited by a certain range such that one knows what sort of evidence verifies or falsifies them. There are situations which can count as Mary's loving me and situations which cannot. But in the case of a theological statement, like "God loves us," there appears to be no delimiting range; for the theist often denies that there are any situations which fall outside the range of "God loves us." If theological statements are irrefutable, how can we learn what meaning is to be attached to them?

Crombie argues that these paradoxical features do not demonstrate the impossibility of meaningful theological statements. On the contrary, recognition of these features contributes to a grasp of the meaning of theological statements. These paradoxical features show one that theological statements are not made about any object which falls within our normal experience. In Crombie's words, they are about a "mystery." There is a sense, it is agreed, in which we cannot know what theological statements are about. This is equivalent to saying that there is a sense in which we cannot know God. However, there is also a sense in which we can know God. The solution to the problem, says Crombie, "must consist in defining the sense in which . . . we can know enough of these things for our speech about them to have an intelligible use." [22] It is the intention of Crombie to portray the meaningfulness of theological statements by showing that these statements are governed by rules which specify what they are about and what they assert about it. This is to be done by a recognition of the fact that language which is apparently homogeneous may exhibit all kinds of logical differences.

[22] I. M. Crombie, "The Possibility of Theological Statements," in *Faith and Logic,* edited by Basil Mitchell (London, 1957), p. 35.

Analysis of these logical differences will portray the meaning of theological statements in spite of their oddity when subjected to the verification principle of the positivists.

Theological statements, then, are factual in spite of their paradoxical characteristics, and this factual meaning can be discovered by analyzing the formal properties of theological statements. One must listen to people making use of theological statements and observe the relationships which hold between these statements and statements of other kinds. For example, although human love and divine love are not to be viewed as identical, nonetheless the fact that the word "love" is chosen for use as a predicate for a theological statement indicates some sort of appropriateness.[23] The nature of human love is to give us some idea of what divine love is like, even though this may not be a precise conception. Human love is an *analogy* which enables us to grasp at least partially the meaning of divine love. Attention to theological language and these analogies enable one to discover the "reference range" of theological statements.

The solution of the skeptic that theological statements appear to have a reference range—that is, that people appear to know what they are talking about when they talk about God because they operate upon the old anthropomorphic conception of a superhuman being in the sky—is unsatisfactory for Crombie. The reference range of theological statements is to be established on more "respectable" grounds. What is this more respectable conception of the divine, and how do we arrive at it? It is the idea of a "compliment which could fill in certain deficiencies in our experience that could not be filled in by further experience or scientific theory making; and its positive content is simply the idea of something (we know not what) which might supply those deficiencies." [24]

It appears that we are back with Locke's "unknowable substance" and perhaps with all the problems that attended this notion. The notion of substance apparently filled a deficiency in Locke's experience. Crombie suggests that the notion of God fulfills a deficiency in our experience, and this notion of a deficiency in our experience is

[23] *Ibid.*, p. 51.
[24] *Ibid.*, p. 56.

quite important in Crombie's attempt to portray the meaning of theological statements.

Crombie's first step in explicating the meaning of this deficiency is to point out "our inability to accept with complete contentment the idea that we are ourselves normal spatio-temporal objects."[25] He feels that part of our experience of ourselves is describable only with the aid of concepts of a nonphysical kind. We are beings with a "limited and imperfect spirituality," and this leads us to think of beings who are spiritually perfect. It is true, Crombie states, that we have no idea of "spirit," but we do have a notion of how the word is used. "We distinguish 'spirit' from 'influenza' or 'digestion' by showing to which aspects of men these words severally infer."[26] Admittedly, the notion of God as a spirit is a "category-transgression." Its logical character is different from that of other abstract nouns. However, this transgression is deliberately committed in order to fulfill this deficiency in our experience. Other concepts applicable to the physical world cannot fulfill this deficiency. In filling this deficiency the notion of a divine spirit has some sort of meaning, though perhaps not "clear and distinct." We have what Crombie calls an "inkling of the reference" of theological statements, or a "hint of the possibility of something we cannot conceive."[27] In talk about God, "what we mean is something rather loose and vague, loosely and vaguely connected with the normal uses of words."[28] The meaning of theological statements like "God is infinite," "God is necessary," and "God is nonderivative" is discovered by noticing the normal uses of words. For example, Crombie tells us, " 'finite' and 'infinite,' 'contingent' and 'necessary,' 'derivative' and 'nonderivative': All these are pairs. . . . The meaning to be attached to the second member of each pair is to be got by seeing what kind of judgement about the world is intended by the use of the first."[29] There is an analogy between the meaning of ordinary predicates and theological predicates. The meaning of theological statements in which these terms are used as predicates cannot be anatomized

[25] *Ibid.*, p. 57.
[26] *Ibid.*, p. 60.
[27] *Ibid.*, p. 58.
[28] *Ibid.*, p. 62.
[29] *Ibid.*, p. 64.

because that which they are about is "inconceivable." However, Crombie says there is a "sense in which we can mean inconceivables." [30] The meaning of this "inconceivable" and such expressions as "Infinite Spirit" stand for "the abstract conception of the possibility of the removal of certain intellectual dissatisfactions which we may feel about the universe of common experience." [31] We are back with the notion of a deficiency in our experience which the notion of God fulfills.

For Crombie propositions about God are to be treated as "parables." There is no literal truth in theological statements, but they do not "mislead as to the nature of the underlying reality." Statements like "God is angry at sin" acquire content by being treated as parables. Parables provide us with analogies, and these analogies between ordinary statements and theological statements portray the meaning of theological statements. Human anger is an "image" of a divine disposition just as is human love. But these analogies enable us only "to see in a glass darkly."

It is clear, then, that Crombie invokes the classical doctrine of analogical predication in order to retain the cognitive significance of theological statements. But he invokes much more. For how are we to know that certain parables refer to God and that others do not? Here he invokes the concept of revelation and authority. "The things we say about God are said on the authority of the words and acts of Christ, who spoke in human language, using parables; and so we too speak of God in parable . . . authoritative parable, authorized parable. . . ." [32] The Christian must be personally committed to the divinity of Christ and trust a *given source* of parables.

Having called upon the doctrine of analogy and upon Christ as the authoritative reference for proper parables, Crombie has one more item up his sleeve to retain the cognitivity of statements about God. He asks: ". . . how do we stand with regard to verification and falsification? Must we, to be making assertions, be prepared to say what could count against them? Let us see how far we can do so. Does anything count decisively against it? No, we reply, because it is true. Could anything count decisively against it? Yes, suffering

[30] *Ibid.*, p. 66.
[31] *Ibid.*
[32] *New Essays*, p. 122.

which was utterly, eternally and irredeemably pointless. Can we then design a crucial experiment? No, because we can never see all of the picture." [33]

That part of the picture which we cannot see now is that part which we shall see in the hereafter. Religious propositions are falsifiable in principle, but for the Christian, "the operation of getting into position to decide" whether a given claim is true or false "is called 'dying' and, though we can all do that, we cannot return to report what we find. By this test, then, religious utterances can be called statements of fact. . . ." [34] Religious assertions such as "God loves us" or "God is merciful" can be falsified in principle, but can never be falsified in practice. Since, however, some conceivable experience, postmortem to be sure, might falsify them, their cognitive status is assured.

Crombie's attempt to defend the factual status of religious utterances, then, is a three-pronged affair: (1) the doctrine of analogy, (2) the authority of Christ, and (3) a theory of eschatological verification. We will comment on all three of these appeals.

First, in regard to the doctrine of analogy, we will not repeat all of the formidable objections which have been posed against this doctrine. We will make just one observation. A meaningful use of analogy is that of taking some characteristic *found in our experience* and postulating a higher degree of that characteristic than is shown in our experience. For example, it is quite meaningful to speak of men attaining a higher degree of knowledge or a higher degree of moral goodness than they now have. It is clear, however, that the religious use of analogy requires much more than differences in degree of some characteristic found in our experience. It requires that the characteristic alluded to in human experience ("love" or "knowledge") be fundamentally different in kind when offered as an attribute of God. The characteristic does not differ merely in degree, for God possesses these qualities in an absolute, *unlimited* sense. He is infinitely good and infinitely wise. This really means that the difference between human goodness and knowledge and divine goodness and knowledge is not one of *degree* but one of *kind*. Since this is the case, the attribution of these infinite qualities

[33] *Ibid.*, p. 124.
[34] *Ibid.*, p. 126.

to God conveys no meaning, for these qualities do not have the experiential grounding required for meaningful comprehension.[35]

Crombie's case, however, rests not solely on the appeal to analogy, but also upon the appeal to the authority of Christ. He states, for example, that "we do not use the analogy to give a sense to 'love' in the theological context. We postulate the analogy because we believe the image to be a faithful image." The faithful image of God's nature is the life and teachings of Christ. One must accept this image, and then the parables become useful in explicating the meaning of theological statements. But does this not mean that one must be "within the faith," so to speak, before analogical statements about God make sense or convey meaning? However, is this not to say merely that theological statements are meaningful to those to whom theological statements are meaningful? This is a far sight from explicating the meaning of theological statements or fixing, in some sense, their "reference-range." Furthermore, if the appeal to analogy fails (as we have argued), then the appeal to *any source* of parable is of no help in fixing the meaning of claims about God, for no matter what the source of parable it always involves reference to *finite, limited* characteristics, and such characteristics can never bridge the gap to meaningful talk about *unlimited, infinite* characteristics.

Let us look briefly at Crombie's theory of eschatological verification as a means of retaining the falsifiability-in-principle of theological statements. His thesis is that religious statements should be treated as hypotheses, to be verified or falsified by reference to data available only after death. Several points must be made about this thesis. First, Crombie rests the factual status of all religious statements upon the truth of this one statement—that there is an afterlife in which additional data will be available. But this statement itself, the claim that one can increase his understanding after death, is a statement which is far from being unproblematic. Some philosophers want to say that it is self-contradictory to speak of "my increased understanding after death," since "death" means the ex-

[35] See my "Religious Language and Analogical Predication," in *The Iliff Review,* Vol. XVII, no. 2 (1960); and Paul Hayner, "Analogical Predication," in *Journal of Philosophy,* Vol. LV (September 25, 1958).

tinction of "me." [36] Such remarks serve to indicate that there is a serious problem with the meaning of the claim that there is an afterlife.

Duff-Forbes argues that the thesis concerning an afterlife is itself a religious claim. Speaking of testing religious beliefs by reference to data provided in the hereafter, he says: ". . . the statement that such a test can be applied to religious utterances, enabling us to say they are factual statements, is itself expressed as one of the religious utterances in question." [37] The circularity that Crombie is involved in on this interpretation becomes obvious: ". . . in order to establish whether or not claims about life after death are factual, true-or-false statements (because religious utterances), we must establish that they are true statements. But this supposes that they *are* factual statements." [38]

Ignoring this difficulty, however, it is clear that the appeal to eschatological verification fails on other grounds. What grounds? Simply these. Even postmortem experience, if there be such, could not be experience of God's unlimited, infinite characteristics. Finite beings cannot have experience of infinite characteristics. Therefore, even if we do have postmortem experiences, we will still be confronted with the same epistemological problems concerning meaningful talk about God.

There is another peculiarity in Crombie's analysis which merits comment. Recall that he claims that from the point of view of verification in practice nothing can count decisively against the assertion that God is merciful. On the other hand, in *principle* the assertion is falsifiable because irredeemably pointless suffering *could* count decisively against it, if we could gather such data (which is not possible in this life). But he also claims that nothing can count decisively against the assertion "because it is true." Now this is odd indeed, for on Crombie's own showing, the data relevant for such a truth claim cannot be had until after death, and then it cannot be reported. The claim "because it is true" is logically precluded given the grounds

[36] John Passmore, "Christianity and Positivism," in *The Australasian Journal of Philosophy*, Vol. 35, no. 2, p. 135.

[37] D. R. Duff-Forbes, *op. cit.*, p. 152.

[38] *Ibid.*, p. 153.

which Crombie cites in defense of the factual status of religious assertions. The most that he can claim is that the issue between the two parties—the one who says pain and suffering prove that God is not merciful, and the other who says that such pain and suffering are compatible with God's mercy and do not invalidate the claim that God is merciful—cannot be settled.

It seems clear, then, that Crombie's attempt to justify the assertion-status of theological statements fails. His attempt fails for three reasons: (1) The doctrine of analogical predication simply will not do the job for which it was devised. (2) He involves himself in circular reasoning, presupposing the assertion-status of some religious claims in arguing for others. (3) The appeal to eschatological verification is of no help in connection with God as infinite being, and it is just such talk about God as infinite being which most perplexes the philosophical analyst.

We conclude that the right-wing response fails to show that key religious statements about God have factual significance.

CHAPTER EIGHT

The Problem of Religious Knowledge

The Problem of Epistemology

This book, it was stated, is concerned with the problem of whether there is religious knowledge. We outlined our procedure for answering this problem in four steps—first, to set forth a criterion enabling us to distinguish religious sentences from sentences of other kinds; second, to set forth criteria for the cognitivity of any given sentence; third, to set forth criteria for the application of the term "knowledge"; and fourth, to discover whether there are religious sentences which are cognitive and which conform to the criteria for knowledge. Thus far we have moved through the first two steps, and we are now in a position to move through steps three and four.

Our answer to the question of whether certain specific religious sentences constitute knowledge is foreordained. This is so because the issue of the cognitivity of a sentence is logically prior to the issue of either its truth or knowledge-status, and, since we have argued that many religious sentences which *purport* to be cognitive (sentences other than exhortations, commands, blessings, and prayers) do not conform to the criteria for cognitivity, the conclusion that they do not conform to the criteria for knowledge is analytic or tautological. However, we have also argued that, within the heterogeneous group of sentences which perform the function we have designated as religious, there are many sentences which do conform to the criteria for cognitivity, since they have some clear literal meaning. Now we must ask if those cognitive sentences conform to the criteria for knowledge.

First, let us observe that some philosophers (especially those who argue that all philosophical problems can be cured by linguistic therapy) might suggest that the problem or question "Is there religious knowledge?" is a pseudo-problem, a problem which can be resolved by a careful consideration of our actual uses of epistemic terms like "know" and "true." There are many different uses of "know," it might be argued. All of them depend on context. No one use is reducible to another. We do, in fact, speak of religious knowledge. The word has an intelligible application in religion. To be sure, the concept "knowledge" may not perform the same function or use in religion as it does (say) in science. But it does have a legitimate use. Our perplexities concerning religious knowledge may stem from the assumption that the concept "knowledge" has but one meaning or use. If we rid ourselves of this initial prejudice and simply look at the various uses this concept has in various areas of discourse, we can rid ourselves of our perplexity.

Such is one possible response to our proposed problem. It amounts to the contention that the problem resolves itself when one recognizes that the term "knowledge" is in fact used in the area of religious discourse, and that this use is one among many. Such a response tends, as it were, to defend the status quo. There is religious knowledge because we use the concept "knowledge" in this connection. In a way this response is peculiar. Aside from the fact that this appeal is to "usage" rather than "use" (to use Ryle's distinction), it is quite obvious that such a response is no therapy to many. Some individuals, for example, even within religion, so to speak, find the question "Is there religious knowledge?" a significant one, being fully aware that the term "knowledge" is used in connection with religion. The fact that the concept is used there does not indicate that it ought to be so used.

We are in agreement with the latter response, which reflects the view that the question "Is there religious knowledge?" cannot be solved simply by *describing* the use or uses of the concept "knowledge." The term "knowledge" is honorific, and many people mistakenly apply it to beliefs which do not warrant the application. Implicit here is a prescriptive or persuasive definition of "knowledge." Some such definition—some set of criteria—is implicitly or explicitly appealed to when this term is applied. Nor need such a definition be arbitrary and philosophically pointless. It can be viewed as one of a series of distinctions which intelligent men have felt impelled to make over the centuries and which they have conceived of as a tool for philosophical clarification.

Our point can be made by looking at the problem in another way. The issue of whether a given sentence is cognitive, we have argued, involves an appeal to a criterion of cognitivity which functions as a norm, and the problem of justifying such a criterion is that of justifying a norm. The same holds true, we are suggesting, for the issue of criteria for knowledge. Whether a given cognitive sentence constitutes knowledge involves an appeal to criteria which function as a norm for the term "knowledge," and the problem of justifying such criteria is that of justifying a norm.

Professor James Oliver has recognized that criteria for the term "knowledge" function normatively. These criteria amount to a set of epistemological rules, and a given sentence is to be characterized as true (or given a certain degree of credibility) if it conforms to those epistemological rules. Oliver argues that criteria for the term "knowledge" or sets of epistemological rules are devised in order to answer the fundamental and central problem of epistemology, namely, "What statements should an individual believe?" He puts the issue in the form of a question: "Why should one be interested in distinguishing what is true from what is false except as a means of deciding what ought to be believed?" [1] The central problem of epistemology is, then, the normative question of which statements one should believe, and hence is a problem in pragmatics. It is concerned with the attitudes of interpreters of a language toward some of the sentences in that language.[2] Professor Oliver does insist that not all sentences are assertions (or "statements," as he puts it) and "there must be some clear meaning for a statement before the question of believing it is considered at all." We have already noted that the question of the cognitivity of a sentence (the question of whether a sentence has "some clear meaning," as Oliver puts it) is

[1] James W. Oliver, "The Problem of Epistemology," *Journal of Philosophy*, Vol. 57, no. 9 (1960), p. 298.

[2] *Ibid.*

logically prior to the issue of the truth of that sentence. Professor Oliver is further insisting that a sentence's having some clear meaning is a logically prior condition for the adoption of *attitudes* of belief or disbelief toward it.

Professor Oliver makes two further observations which result in a modified formulation of what he takes to be the central problem of epistemology. First, he points out that, although Descartes and the rationalists generally have advocated views involving only two attitudes of belief—complete certainty and complete disbelief—people can and do take a wide range of attitudes or degrees of belief toward statements. Thus one problem, important but subordinate to the central problem of epistemology, is that of providing a useful scale of degrees of belief. Secondly, a comprehensive classification of statements is needed so that there can be a separate and adequate discussion of all issues of concern to epistemologists. He notes that we have at present classifications among analytic, synthetic, and self-contradictory statements; among universal, existential, and singular statements; and among statements in various levels of language. Distinctions have been made among statements purporting to refer to phenomena, those purporting to refer to abstract entities, and those purporting to refer to supernatural beings. A comprehensive classification of all statements is a problem preliminary to the solution of the central problem of epistemology—what should an individual believe? These two observations, the need for a scale of degrees of belief and the need for a comprehensive classification of all statements, leads Professor Oliver to the following modified formulation of the central problem of epistemology: "What degrees of belief should an individual accord to clear literal statements of various kinds?" [3]

We are in fundamental agreement with Professor Oliver's formulation of the central problem of epistemology. The goal of the epistemologist is to enable one to decide what he ought to believe. And since there are different kinds of statements with different kinds and amounts of evidence relevant to them, it is the task of epistemology to assist one in discovering which attitude (in a scale including belief, disbelief, no opinion, etc.) is the appropriate attitude to

[3] *Ibid.*, p. 300.

adopt toward any given statement. Specifically in regard to sentences which perform the function which we have designated as religious, it is the task of the epistemologist to assist us in discovering which attitude (in a scale including belief, disbelief, no opinion, etc.) is the appropriate attitude to adopt toward a given religious sentence. The formulation of this scale of belief and a comprehensive classification of all religious sentences which are cognitive or which have "some clear meaning" is required before the epistemologist can help us ascertain which attitude is the appropriate one to adopt toward a *given* religious sentence. It is impossible for the epistemologist to perform this function in regard to sentences which have no clear meaning. We have already noted that the formulation of a criterion of cognitivity or a criterion of "clarity" ("some clear meaning"), as Professor Oliver puts it, is also a task logically prior to the performance of the central task of the epistemologist.

Our problem in this chapter can now be clearly stated. We have a classification of cognitive religious sentences which includes descriptive sentences, predictive sentences, explanations, historical sentences, and autobiographical sentences. We will also assume that there is a scale of attitudes (including the attitudes of belief, disbelief, no opinion, and other intermediate attitudes) which one may adopt toward any given cognitive religious sentence. Our task is to provide a scheme by virtue of which one can decide which attitude is the appropriate one to adopt toward any given cognitive religious sentence. Answering this question is tantamount to answering the question of whether there is religious knowledge, for I take the phrase "religious knowledge" to designate cognitive religious sentences toward which it is appropriate to adopt an attitude of belief. Admittedly, there may be different degrees of belief appropriate to different religious sentences, depending on the kind and amount of evidence adduced. Thus, the phrase "religious knowledge" may not have completely clear-cut boundaries. However, this fact need not be bothersome. We can set up criteria conformity to which would make a given cognitive religious sentence one toward which it would be appropriate to adopt a very strong attitude of belief, one of almost complete certainty. Cognitive religious sentences which conform strictly to these criteria would be classified as "highly probable knowledge." Those which do not conform so strictly would be classified differently—perhaps "probable knowledge." One would want to have a number of degrees of probability, and hence a number of degrees of the attitude of belief appropriately corresponding to the degree of probability.

In order to accomplish this we need to do three things. First, we must set forth a criterion or a set of criteria for the term "knowledge." Secondly, we must give justifying reasons for adopting that criterion or set of criteria. We have already noted that these criteria will serve as a norm by which to judge if any given cognitive religious sentence constitutes knowledge, just as a criterion for cognitivity serves as a norm for deciding whether a given religious sentence is cognitive. We have also noted the difficulties in justifying a criterion of cognitivity, but we did offer such a criterion and gave reasons for accepting it. We must also offer reasons for accepting our criteria for the term "knowledge."

We agree at the outset that any formulated criteria for knowledge are normative principles or rules which cannot themselves be confirmed as either true or false, as can statements which conform to these criteria. Regardless of this fact, however, sound reasons can be given for the adoption of given criteria delineating the term "knowledge." Having set forth criteria for the term "knowledge" and having given reasons for the adoption of those criteria, we, thirdly, will apply those criteria to sentences denominated as both cognitive and religious and see if they conform to it. This will necessitate an analysis of the kind and amount of evidence adduced for given religious sentences. We obviously cannot do this for all religious sentences, but we will do it with a sufficient number to make clear the framework for answering the question of whether any given religious sentence constitutes knowledge.

Criteria for Knowledge

What criteria, then, are we to adopt for the term "knowledge?" There are three classical requirements often set forth for the proper application of this term. A. J. Ayer, in his *The Problem of Knowledge,* argues for these three criteria, concluding that "necessary and sufficient conditions for knowing that something is the case are first that what one is said to know be true, secondly that one be sure of it, and thirdly that one should have the right to be sure." [4] We will use Ayer's position as a point of reference in developing our requirements for the use of the term "knowledge."

Let us see what leads Ayer to formulate these criteria. His first criterion for knowledge is that the proposition that one knows actually be true. His reason for insisting on this requirement is simply that we cannot be said to know if the proposition of which we are fully confident turns out to be false. "There would be a contradiction in saying both that he knew the statement to be true and that it was false; but, this is because it enters into the meaning of the word 'know' that one cannot know what is not true." [5] Knowledge cannot be of what is false unless it is knowledge of the true proposition that a proposition is false. Ayer's position on truth is that a statement is true "if the situation which it describes is as it describes it," a version of the correspondence theory.

Ayer's second requirement is that "one be sure" of one's belief, or that one's belief be "fully confident." This criterion is required, it seems, on the grounds that the existence of knowledge analytically entails a knowing subject—one who has an attitude toward a proposition or state of affairs. One cannot say, "I know x but I am not sure of x." That a proposition is true does not entail *knowing* that it is true, but that a proposition constitutes knowledge does entail an epistemic attitude of certainty toward that proposition on the part of the owner. (Recently this requirement has been seriously questioned in a detailed essay by Professor Woozley. Woozley argues that one may know something to be the case while being unsure of it.)[6]

Ayer's third requirement for knowledge is that one have the "right to be sure" of the proposition confidently believed. One has the right if he arrives at his belief by a process of reasoning which would be "generally reliable." He himself admits that the process of arriving at a belief through "generally reliable" methods will

[4] A. J. Ayer, *The Problem of Knowledge* (London: The Macmillan Co., Ltd.), p. 35.

[5] *Ibid.*, p. 19.

[6] A. D. Woozley. "Knowing and Not Knowing," in *Aristotelian Society Proceeding,* New Series, Vol. 53 (1952-53).

vary from one instance to another. "Claims to know empirical statements may be upheld by a reference to perception, or to memory, or to testimony, or to historical records, or to scientific laws. But such backing is not always strong enough for knowledge. Whether it is so or not depends upon the circumstances of the particular case. . . . In a given instance it is possible to decide whether the backing is strong enough to justify a claim to knowledge. But to say in general how strong it has to be would require our drawing up a list of the conditions under which perception, or memory, or other forms of evidence are reliable. And this would be a very complicated matter, if indeed it could be done at all." [7] The requirement, then, that one have the right to be sure is left vague, and necessarily so, Ayer claims. Stated roughly, one has the right to be sure of a belief if that belief is arrived at through generally reliable methods and if the data collected by those methods strongly support that belief.

Now all three of these conditions must be fulfilled, Ayer claims, if one is to be said to have knowledge. The first requirement—that one be sure or be in a certain mental state—is not in itself a necessary and sufficient condition for knowledge, because however firm one's conviction be that a proposition is true, it does not logically follow that that proposition is true. In fact, both the first and second conditions may be fulfilled and knowledge yet be lacking. That is, one may feel confident that a belief is true, and the belief may be true, and still that belief may not constitute knowledge, for one may not have reliable evidence or the right to be sure that the belief is true. Furthermore, the satisfaction of the first and third requirements—having the attitude of certainty and having the right to be sure—is not sufficient for Ayer; for even if these conditions prevail the proposition believed may turn out to be false. For these reasons, Ayer insists that all three conditions must be satisfied for the term "knowledge" to be appropriately applied.

This problem, however, arises: Can we ever know whether condition one, that the proposition which one believes be true, is satisfied? Especially in the case of purported factual knowledge, is it not always logically possible that future data, data which one does not and

[7] A. J. Ayer, *op. cit.*, pp. 31-32.

cannot have at the time of one's judgment, will turn out to be disconfirming? Suppose, for example that a given proposition at an early stage in the development of science were extremely well supported by the evidence then at hand. Suppose that the same proposition at a later stage were highly disconfirmed by empirical findings. Would we say that the proposition at the earlier stage was true but that it was false at the later stage? Ayer's answer to this, I think, would be no. It would be more appropriate to say that on the basis of the initial evidence the proposition had been quite probable, but that the more recent empirical findings make it highly probable that the proposition is not true. Concerning purported claims to factual knowledge, it must always be kept in mind that although present empirical findings make a given proposition highly probable, future developments in science and future empirical findings may tend to disconfirm that proposition. Since that is the case, one can never know concerning most factual claims whether they are true for good and all. At best, one can say that a given factual proposition is highly probable.

Since this is the case, it would seem that we could never know if criterion one were ever satisfied, for Ayer's requirement that the proposition believed be true to constitute knowledge seems to be a requirement that the proposition be true for good and all—that if a proposition is true and constitutes knowledge no future data can possibly disconfirm it. His reason for insisting upon this requirement is what he calls the "linguistic fact that what is not true cannot properly be said to be known." [8] His appeal is apparently to the way that the term "knowledge" is used in discourse, and his claim is that if it is used in such a manner it is self-contradictory for a proposition to constitute knowledge and yet be false. His claim is, I think, true of some uses of the term "knowledge." But, of course, there are many uses of this term. And even when it is used in the sense of "knowing that" something is the case, the meaning is often that the proposition believed is well supported by all the evidence at hand at that time and place—not that the proposition believed is true for good and all.

[8] *Ibid.*, p. 25.

Although the difficulties which we have suggested concerning criterion one arise if one accepts Ayer's criteria for the term "knowledge"—the difficulty being that we can never know, for most factual claims, whether they are true—this does not mean that we can never have knowledge. That is, this difficulty need not lead us in the direction of the skeptic who claims that "we do not strictly know anything at all." The assumption that it does is based on adding a fourth criterion to Ayer's three, namely, that we must know that we know. The traditional Cartesian rationalist insisted on this requirement, the consequence being that only a very few beliefs or statements could constitute knowledge, statements which assert nothing more than the content of one's immediate consciousness (to which no future data are relevant) and statements which are now generally characterized as analytic.

Recently, Norman Malcolm has argued that in addition to statements describing the content of one's consciousness, some statements about physical objects, such as "Here is an ink bottle," constitute knowledge in the sense that the grounds for one's belief are conclusive. They are conclusive not because future evidence is irrelevant to the truth of the belief, but because one's evidence or grounds are so good that future evidence, though relevant, could never possibly refute the belief.[9] Malcolm's position would seem to imply that for a wide range of beliefs we could know that those beliefs are true and actually know that we know.

Two points might be made here. First, it may be seriously questioned that there can be a guarantee that certain beliefs (including physical-object statements) will not be refuted by possible future experiences bearing on their truth. Secondly, even if Malcolm is correct, in which case the insistence upon knowing that we know as a requirement for knowledge would not lead us to skepticism, we need not accept this requirement. In fact, if Professor Adams is correct, as I am inclined to believe, those philosophers who have insisted on this requirement have done so because, in their analyses of what it is to know, they "have concentrated on the sentence 'I know that *p*' rather than 'He (or you) knows(s) that *p*' and this leads to the con-

[9] Norman Malcolm, "Knowledge and Belief," in *Mind,* Vol. 61, no. 242 (April, 1952).

fusion . . . of knowing that *p* with claiming to know *p*." [10] Adams gives this analysis:

> When I say, "This pencil is red," I claim to know that it is red, even though I do not say that I know it. It is perfectly appropriate in such a case for someone to ask, "How do you know that it is?" It would be a linguistic absurdity to say, "This pencil really is red but I don't know that it is." Nevertheless the truth of "The pencil is red" in no sense requires the truth of "I know that the pencil is red." There are two distinct problems: (1) the truth-conditions of the statement and (2) the justificatory conditions of saying it. With regard to "I know that this pencil is red," it is difficult to keep them distinct. Although the truth-conditions of the statement are exactly the same as those of the sentence "E. M. A. knows that this pencil is red," one is likely to ask for the justificatory conditions of my saying it along with a query about its truth-conditions. And my claim to know what I have asserted is valid only if I know that this pencil is red. Hence the confusion of the justificatory condition of saying it with the truth-conditions of what is said leads one to analyze the truth-conditions of "I know that I know that p" for those of "I know that p." This is why, I think, that it is held that knowing that p involves knowing that you know that p." [11]

We find Ayer's criteria for "knowledge" acceptable with this qualification—that we distinguish between knowledge in a pure sense and justified knowledge claims. Knowledge in the pure sense requires the classical criteria advocated by Ayer. In particular "*p* constitutes knowledge" here implies that *p* could *never* turn out to be false. This is, of course, a very strong sense of the term "knowledge." Nonetheless, there could be many beliefs which fulfill this condition, even if we cannot know that they fulfill it. A justified knowledge claim, on the other hand, is a claim or belief for which one has "good grounds," a belief which is strongly supported by the evidence available. This is a weaker sense of "know," in which that which one knows may turn out to be false. That a given claim is justified depends on the kind of claim being made and the kind

[10] E. M. Adams, "On Knowing That," in *The Philosophical Quarterly,* Vol. 8 (1958), pp. 304-305.

[11] *Ibid.,* p. 305.

and amount of evidence supporting it. But certain methodological requirements, requirements which function as norms, must be followed in the collection and interpretation of data. Those methodological requirements consist in the established canons of inductive and deductive logic. If one uses these methods, and if one's belief is supported by the data collected and interpreted by virtue of these reliable methods, then one's belief may be appropriately classified as knowledge or claimed to be knowledge. This does not assure, however, that that belief constitutes knowledge in the strong sense. We see no reason why both of these uses of "know" cannot be retained, as long as they are not confused. It may be the case that human beings, for the most part, must be content with knowledge in the weak sense. This fact does not preclude, however, that we have a great deal of knowledge in the strong sense. Nor does it mean that we are led down the road to skepticism.

What justifying grounds do we have for adopting our proposed criteria for knowledge—the methodological requirements cited above? We cannot say that these criteria are themselves true or false or constitute knowledge. However, we can give pragmatic reasons for adopting them. In the first place, the use of these criteria has proven fruitful in practice, enabling us to make predictions and in general to adjust to our environment. Secondly, we have argued that the principal problem of epistemology is that of enabling one to decide what degrees of belief one should accord to cognitive statements (statements with "some clear meaning") of various kinds. It is our contention that the above criteria for knowledge enable individuals to solve this problem. Adoption of these criteria enables one to ascertain the degree of probability of different beliefs and to adjust one's degree of belief proportionately according to the evidence. Such adoption also offers the advantage of intersubjective agreement on the propositions tested. Furthermore, the application of these criteria to purported factual statements is a continually self-correcting procedure, the very opposite of dogmatism. And finally, adoption of those criteria and methods yields a body of logically consistent beliefs.

Now, admittedly, the force of the latter pragmatic or vindicating reasons depends upon the acceptance of our characterization of the central problem of epistemology and the desirability of adjusting one's degree of belief proportionately according to the evidence. If one takes the central problem of epistemology to be that of making individuals happy with what beliefs they have, the goal being the adjustment of one's beliefs according to the degree of happiness provided, then the above pragmatic reasons will have no force. This concern with happiness seems to be the test for adjusting beliefs for many people. Others, including a number of theologians, operate on the assumption that one's beliefs (specifically religious beliefs) should be accepted on sheer unexamined faith, the attempt to adjust one's beliefs according to the evidence being an instance of man's prideful and sinful nature. Here there is a complete parting of the ways, for this amounts to saying that there is no problem of epistemology in the sense that we have defined it. If one does not accept the goals of proportioning one's beliefs according to the available evidence and attaining a body of logically consistent beliefs, then our justifying reasons for our proposed criteria for knowledge have no force and the criteria themselves will not be denominated as "good" criteria. When this occurs, however, all rational dispute must cease, for what is meant by a rational person is one who does proportion his beliefs according to the available evidence. There is no question that many theologians, by their own admission,[12] are asking us to believe that which is irrational. The issue in the last analysis is that of whether one wants to be rational or irrational in his beliefs. There are, however, some theologians (empirical theologians in particular) who accept our characterization of the central problem of epistemology and the desirability of proportioning one's beliefs according to the available evidence. With these persons at least, our proposed criteria for knowledge (and the vindicating reasons for those criteria) are acceptable, and rational disputation remains possible.

Formal Knowledge and Factual Knowledge

Along with the above criteria for the term "knowledge," I propose that we make a distinction between two essentially differ-

[12] See my remarks on Emil Brunner and Soren Kierkegaard in Chapter Five.

ent kinds of knowledge—formal knowledge and factual knowledge. Although few religious claims are set forth as constituting formal knowledge, this distinction is a useful classificatory device, for at least some religious claims, when analyzed, turn out to be formal truths. This distinction, of course, is a very old one, and it itself involves a number of epistemological problems. The entire analytic-synthetic controversy[13] of the past thirty years centers around this distinction. For now, however, we will ignore these problems, for a consideration of them would lead us away from our present concern into very specialized problems in epistemology. We will admit that one's answers to the problems centering around the analytic-synthetic distinction have a crucial bearing on one's theory of knowledge, but this is not the place to set forth a theory about this distinction.

Let us set forth the criteria for formal knowledge first. This kind of knowledge is exemplified in logic, mathematics, and geometry. It provides no information about facts in the world. Formal knowledge is the result of the acceptance of a set of postulates, rules of justification or proof rules (for example, *modus ponens* in logic), and the consequent deduction of a conclusion in accordance with that set of postulates and proof rules. The term "valid," rather than the term "true," is often applied to conclusions which are obtained in this manner.

Some philosophers contend that there can be several logical systems depending on the set of postulates and proof rules accepted. Geometricians also contend that there can be a number of systems of geometry depending on one's initial postulates and proof rules. Such alternative geometrical systems have in fact been devised, so that we now have Riemannian and Lobachevskian geometries[14] as well as

[13] See, for example, W. V. O. Quine's article, "Two Dogmas of Empiricism," in *From a Logical Point of View* (New York: Oxford University Press, 1953), and Morton White, "The Analytic and Synthetic: An Untenable Dualism," in *John Dewey: Philosopher of Science and Freedom,* edited by Sidney Hook (New York: The Dial Press, Inc., 1950) For a defense of the analytic-synthetic distinction and a reply to Quine, see H. P. Grice and P. F. Strawson, "In Defense of a Dogma," in *Philosophical Review,* Vol. 65, no. 2 (April, 1956).

[14] See Henri Poincaré, *Science and Hypothesis,* translated by G. B. Halsted (New York, 1905), Chapters III and V. Reprinted in *Readings in the Philosophy of Science,* edited by Herbert Feigl and May Brodbeck (New York: Appleton-Century-Crofts, Inc., 1953), pp. 171-180.

Euclidean geometry. The possibility of the formulation of these different systems of formal knowledge gives rise to the problem of choosing one system (one set of postulates and proof rules) rather than others. I know of no justifying reasons for such a choice other than the internal consistency and completeness of a given system, or the fact that acceptance of one system rather than another has certain desirable pragmatic consequences.

Formal knowledge, then, always conforms to the following criteria. It makes no reference to nature or facts in the world (though it may be "applied" to facts in the world). It is absolutely certain, given the postulates, rules of justification, and the moves appropriate to those postulates and rules; and a denial of a conclusion which follows rigorously from an accepted set of postulates according to the proof rules involves one in a self-contradiction. Conclusions of such rigorous reasoning are generally not true or false in the usual sense of "true" or "false," but rather valid or invalid. In cases in which one's premises are true, a rigorous conclusion may be both valid and true; this is often the case in logic. But the postulates of one's formal system (logic, geometry, or mathematics) are not themselves true or false, but pragmatically justified. They are convenient for certain reasons—or they may be arbitrary. And, as noted, there may be alternative systems of formal knowledge.

The criteria for factual knowledge are quite different. Factual knowledge is always informative about the world. It includes descriptions and explanations of the phenomena of nature. It is inferential and testable; however, the testing procedures can at best render factual inferences highly probable, never completely certain. Even if the present available evidence completely supports a given factual belief, there is always the possibility that some important data have been overlooked, and the further possibility that future experience will provide disconfirming data.[15]

The testing procedures for factual claims are numerous and vari-

[15] One exception to this is what Bertrand Russell calls "basic propositions" and what have been called "protocol sentences." These are descriptions of one's immediate, transitory sense data and make no claim to which future data are relevant. See Bertrand Russell's *Human Knowledge: Its Scope and Limits* (New York: Simon & Schuster, Inc., 1948); and A. J. Ayer, "Basic Propositions," in *Philosophical Analysis*, edited by Max Black (Ithaca, New York: Cornell University Press, 1950).

ous, differing according to subject matter and kinds of evidence. Observation, testimonies, memories, and statistical data are types of evidence for factual beliefs, and each type of evidence presents different evaluation problems. There are factors which increase or decrease the reliability of evidence of each type; and, in testing a belief, appropriate precautions must be taken in gathering and evaluating evidence of different kinds. When these precautions are taken and the available evidence is reliable, and when that evidence supports a given belief or hypothesis—there being no disconfirming evidence at the time—then we are justified in maintaining that that belief or hypothesis is highly probable and constitutes knowledge. If most of the evidence supports the belief but there is some evidence which tends to be disconfirming, then we are still justified in maintaining that the belief is true; however, the degree of probability is proportionately less and one's attitude of belief should be proportionately less intense. A factual belief that conforms to these criteria and hence constitutes a justified knowledge claim at one given time may later not conform to these criteria; it would then no longer be a justified claim.

The Appeal to Religious Experience

Having set forth criteria for knowledge, and having given vindicating reasons for these criteria, we are now in a position to ask whether the sentences which we denominated as both cognitive and religious conform to these criteria. This will require an analysis of the kind and amount of evidence adduced for any given such sentence. As might be expected, this analysis will result in a rejection of a number of criteria for knowledge incompatible with those we have adopted.

A logical consequence of the acceptance of our proposed criteria for knowledge is that any cognitive religious sentence which bases its claim to truth on a private, subjective, immediate experience does not constitute knowledge. Bertrand Russell [16] has characterized

[16] Bertrand Russell, *The Problems of Philosophy,* Seventeenth Impression (London: Oxford University Press, 1943), p. 46. First published in 1912.

such private, immediate experience as "knowledge by acquaintance." This "knowledge by acquaintance" is simply awareness of one's direct experience with no interpretations as yet placed on that direct experience. It includes awareness of one's sense-data, feelings, moods, attitudes, and emotions. G. I. Lewis calls such experience "the given" or "awareness of the directly presented." [17] It is neither true nor false. Only statements *about* this experience or statements about what the experience is of can be true or false. In the case of many interpretations placed on experiences, there are procedural devices and rules of justifications which can render those interpretations true or false. Such interpretations are based on intersubjectively testable evidence. However, when no claim is made about an experience, or when claims are made about an experience but there are no procedural devices and rules of justification for testing the claims, one can hardly speak of such experience or claims about that experience as knowledge.

Many cognitive religious sentences are based exactly on this appeal, namely, a claim about a direct and immediate experience which cannot be publicly tested. When, for example, the truth of the sentence "God exists" rests upon "personal religious experience" or "mystical religious experience" or "revelation" (something purportedly revealed to someone in a direct experience), there are no intersubjective testing procedures for checking such claims. If the sentence "God exists" is testable at all when its truth is based on this kind of direct experience, the meaning of the sentence "God exists" is reduced to the assertion "I have an experience of such and such a kind." If the meaning of the sentence "God exists" is reduced to the assertion that one is having a particular kind of experience, feeling, or emotion, then that sentence may constitute knowledge if testing procedures show that it is probable that that person is having a certain kind of emotional experience or feeling. However, the religious believer will not permit the meaning of the religious sentence "God exists" to be reduced in this manner. He insists that the claim makes reference to something *of which* he has direct experience, not simply to the fact that he is having an experience. Since there are no

[17] C. I. Lewis, *An Analysis of Knowledge and Valuation* (Lasalle, Illinois: The Open Court Publishing Co., 1946), p. 24.

intersubjective testing procedures for this claim, it cannot be classified as knowledge, even if the sentence is given some clear meaning and it happens to be a true sentence. In fact, to the extent that the meaning of the religious sentence "God exists" (for the mystic, for one who appeals to "religious experience," or for one who appeals to "revelation") is not reducible to the assertion that one is having a given experience (a claim which might be tested), the problem of the cognitive significance of that sentence arises again.

Rudolf Otto, for example, appeals to religious experience as evidence of God's existence.[18] The religious experience is what he calls a "numinous feeling." Through this "numinous feeling," which he characterizes as a "unique original feeling-response," he claims that one is able to apprehend the existence of a corresponding "numinous object," which he calls the "mysterium tremendum." He admits that the "mysterium tremendum" is beyond all conceptual understanding. However, if God, or the "mysterium tremendum," is beyond all conceptual understanding, and if the meaning of the sentence "God exists" is not reducible to a sentence stating that one has certain feelings (feelings of "awe," etc.), then there is a serious question as to what the sentence is about and the extent of the claim being made. Under these conditions, religious sentences, which for Otto are purportedly cognitive, do not conform to our criterion for cognitivity. For example, Otto insists upon applying the predicates "absolute goodness" and "absolute power" to God. But if God is beyond all conceptual understanding and no merely human concepts are applicable to Him, then no clear meaning can be given such sentences. We have already noted that the doctrine of analogical predication fails to help at this point.

Those who appeal to religious experience as grounds for religious beliefs are involved, then, in some problems. If religious sentences based on this appeal are reducible in meaning to assertions that one has certain kinds of feelings, emotions, sensations, or attitudes, then those sentences are cognitively meaningful. These would be testable claims and may conform to our criteria for knowledge. Interpreted this way, however, these religious sentences lose their objective im-

[18] Rudolf Otto, *The Idea of the Holy*, translated by John W. Harvey (London, 1924).

port. That is, they no longer are viewed as making claims about something other than a subjective feeling or emotion, i.e., an externally existing being of some sort. If, however, those who base their religious beliefs on this appeal to "religious experience" deny that their beliefs or sentences are reducible to autobiographical statements of feeling, then they must specify the nature and extent of the claims that they are making if those religious sentences are to be viewed as being cognitive. Since they agree at the outset that no human concepts are applicable to God, and since the doctrine of analogical predication fails them, it would appear that, interpreted this way, their purported claims about God are noncognitive.

If, on the other hand, it is claimed that religious experience is a guarantee of *both* the cognitivity and the truth of these religious claims, then we can only point out that sentences based on this appeal do not conform to the criteria for knowledge for which we have argued. We may point out the advantages of our proposed criteria for knowledge and the disadvantages of the assumption that experience is a guarantee of its own validity. Clearly, if experience is taken as a guarantee of its own validity, then there is no way of distinguishing knowledge claims which are credible from those which are not, and hence no way of solving the central problem of epistemology, namely, what degree of belief one should accord to cognitive sentences of various kinds. Admittedly, these reasons for adopting our criteria for knowledge are not logically coercive.

If it is claimed that religious experience is a special kind of knowledge requiring no testing, whereas *other* kinds of experience must be tested to constitute knowledge, then this claim, it seems to me, must be justified. Furthermore, even assuming this claim to be correct, the believer is left in the position of having to accept all religious claims based on this appeal as being true, for there are no rules of justification which enable him to distinguish true religious claims from false ones or veridical religious experiences from nonveridical ones. One would even have to accept religious sentences which are self-contradictory, for there are such sentences which are based on the appeal to religious experience.

Up to this point we have argued that religious sentences based on the appeal to religious experience cannot be classified as knowledge if those sentences purport to make claims about something other than the fact that individuals have had certain experiences. In a somewhat oversimplified fashion we classified both the appeal of the religious mystic and the appeal to revelation under the appeal to religious experience. There are, of course, different kinds of religious mystics—Christian mystics who insist on saying very definite things about God who exists objectively, and Buddhist mystics who insist that their religious sentences refer only to their religious experience and who make no predications of God. In the last analysis, however, all mystics, those who insist on speaking and those who do not, maintain that they have a direct awareness or experience of God, and we are maintaining that the appeal to this experience in any case does not constitute *knowledge* of God. We classified the appeal to revelation under that of religious experience because any revelation must be a revelation to some individual or group of individuals in a personal experience. Even the claim that a given book is a revelation of God requires reference to the revelation first being given someone in his personal experience and then being put into words in a book. All religious sentences, then, which purport to have objective import and which have as their justifying grounds merely "religious experience" cannot be classified as knowledge. This includes the claims not only that God exists, but that Christ is his son, that one's soul is immortal, that there is a heaven for those who obey God and a hell for those who sin, that Christ will return to earth, etc. And to the extent that any religious sentence based on this appeal cannot be given some clear meaning so that the speaker and the hearer can know or find out what the sentence is about and the extent of the claim being made about it, the issue of the cognitivity of these sentences arises again.

We have noted that some thinkers maintain that religious claims are not to be taken literally but symbolically. Religious sentences, it is argued, are false when taken literally but true when understood symbolically. We also noted that this appeal to the symbolic, non-literal truth of religious claims often is based on the acceptance of the doctrine of analogical predication, a doctrine we found wanting. Without again raising the question of whether these so-called "symbolic" religious sentences are cognitive, we might note that in the last analysis the claim that religious sentences are "symbolically true" is based on the appeal to religious experience. For it is often maintained that in order to grasp the meaning and see the truth of these sentences which function symbolically, one must have had the kind of experience which these sentences symbolize. Immediately the question of the testability of those experiences (the issue of whether they are veridical) which form the basis for these so-called "symbolic" religious truths arises. The appeal to "symbolic truth" then faces the same problems which face the appeal to "religious experience" as grounds for religious belief.

Subjectivity and Religious Knowledge: Augustine, Kierkegaard, and Tillich

(a) Special mention must be made of the approach to the problem of religious knowledge of those who accept the Augustinian epistemology. Augustine declared that "faith precedes reason" because *nisi credideritis, non intelligetis*—unless you believe you will not understand.[19] This position is undergoing current rejuvenation. As one exponent puts it, "The time has surely come for Christian philosophy to be frankly Augustinian again and call in Christian faith to liberate reason from the toils of rationalism and its corollary, skepticism." [20]

Actually there is some problem in specifying exactly what is meant by the Augustinian dictum that "faith precedes reason." Faith is apparently not to be taken merely as intellectual assent to certain scriptural propositions. It is "the awakening of the mind to truth, a new way of seeing things, a means of understanding what before did not make sense, the acquiring of categories of interpretation by means of which our whole experience and thought become rational and coherent." [21] Having faith, or this "new way of seeing things" and "a means of understanding what before did not make sense," is dependent upon the state of one's will. As Robert Cushman puts it, the Augustinian principle that faith precedes reason

[19] St. Augustine, *Enchirird,* V, in *Nicene and Post-Nicene Fathers,* ed. by Philip Schaff (New York, 1900).

[20] Alan Richardson, *Christian Apologetics* (New York: Harper & Row, Publishers, 1947), p. 242.

[21] *Ibid.,* p. 238.

is "the doctrine of the primacy of the will in all knowledge. What is known cannot be divorced from what is loved. At the very minimum, all cognition is directly dependent upon interest, nor is anything fully known to which the consent of the will has not been given." [22] On another occasion he states: "Augustine perceived in the merely rational approach to God an internal contradiction: it cannot reach God because it does not want to have God. It withholds commitment until it has sight; but it cannot achieve sight until it yields commitment. The rational approach to God does not perceive that it founders upon the original sinfulness of the human heart." [23]

In this appeal faith fundamentally involves the acceptance of the doctrine of Incarnation. For Augustine the Incarnation is that which gives meaning to history, and ultimate reality can be apprehended rightly only through a particular historical event, namely, Jesus Christ.[24] Faith in the Incarnation provides what Richardson calls a "category of interpretation by means of which our whole experience and thought become rational and whole," or, in the words of Cushman, "the true first principium of knowledge, and the adequate starting-point for the interpretation of the totality of human experience." Faith (involving acceptance of the doctrine of Incarnation) is the "indispensable corrective of a reason disabled by sinful pride."

Assuming the above, brief as it is, to be a not inaccurate statement of the Augustinian position, let us set forth some of the problems it presents to one concerned with whether there is religious knowledge. First, it appears on occasion that faith for the Augustinian *is* a kind of knowing. Richardson remarks that the person with faith "sees the truth to which he was formerly blind," and that faith provides a "source of illumination." Augustine himself speaks of "seeing God"—*intellectualis visio Dei.* This language suggests that faith itself is an avenue of cognition—that one can have an immediate apprehension of God. Interpreted thus the Augustinian position amounts to an appeal to "religious experience" or "religious

[22] Robert Cushman, "Faith and Reason in the Thought of St. Augustine," *Church History,* 19, no. 4 (December, 1956), p. 273.

[23] *Ibid.,* p. 285.

[24] *Ibid.,* p. 272.

intuition," an appeal which we have examined and found seriously wanting. At least some who accept the Augustinian position, however, maintain that this is not the proper interpretation of "faith." Faith is not a way of knowing.[25]

If faith is not a way of knowing but a necessary condition for knowing, let us ask the question, does the Augustinian doctrine mean that, if one wholeheartedly accepts a belief (like the doctrine of Incarnation), then reason can and does justify that belief as knowledge? It would seem that the acceptance of a belief would have nothing to do with whether the evidence supported that belief. Such acceptance might have the value of making one at least consider the belief as a hypothesis, but it is more likely that if one wholeheartedly accepted a belief it would function not as a hypothesis but as a dogma. Surely, however, we cannot assume that the mere acceptance of a belief makes it possible for reason to justify that belief as knowledge.

Richardson states, for example, that "our knowledge of God in this life is essentially a rational knowing made possible by faith in the biblical revelation." [26] He is making a distinction here between "faith" and "rational knowing." The former is a necessary condition for the latter, but presumably not a sufficient condition. What more is needed? Well, it would seem that evidence must be cited to support the proposition accepted on faith in order for it to be an instance of "rational knowing." My question is this: Could one have "faith in the biblical revelation" even though the evidence be such that one's belief or beliefs based on this faith would be interpreted as *not* constituting knowledge? This question must be answered affirmatively if there is to be a genuine distinction between "faith" and "rational knowing," and yet one wonders if the religious believer could give an unqualified affirmative answer to this question. One wonders what answer the Augustinian would give. Would he maintain that having "faith in biblical revelation" entails placing only *one* justifiable interpretation on certain occurrences or data, and hence that the belief accepted on faith also is known rationally (supported by data)? It often seems that this is the case. But this is a

[25] Richardson, *op. cit.*, p. 244.
[26] *Ibid.*, p. 243.

way of saying that beliefs based on "faith in biblical revelation" *must* be ("must" in the sense of logical necessity) rational. If this is maintained one wonders what has happened to the distinction between "faith" and "rational knowing." Is it not obliterated? And if so, is not the Augustinian left in the uncomfortable position of maintaining that "faith" is both a necessary and sufficient condition for knowing?

This critical point can be re-enforced by an analysis of the claim that the reason of human beings is "disabled by sinful pride." One wonders if this claim is meant to be taken as a descriptive statement or as a moral or normative judgment. But if it is to be taken as either a descriptive thesis or a normative one, surely we need criteria for the phrase "disabled by sinful pride." Now what are these criteria for the Augustinian? Cushman gives us some help. He characterizes the Augustinian account of man's prideful will in this manner. "To man's awareness all reality is given, the temporal and the eternal. But in virtue of his fallen condition man is turned from the Light to the creatures made luminous by the Light. The turned back is symbolic of the perverted love (original sin). Therefore the order of creatures becomes the dominant object of knowledge in virtue of the coercive inclination of man's will. What else is love (caritas) except will, asks Augustine. When this will is directed toward the creatures, the inclination towards God and, therefore, the awareness of God, diminishes. It declines in proportion to the liveliness of man's concupiscence toward the world of the senses." [27]

There are several theological notions in this passage—the notion of man's "fallen condition," the doctrine of original sin, and the notion of "Light"—all closely connected with the Augustinian view of man's prideful will. But a "prideful will" is apparently one in which the inclination towards God and the awareness of God are diminished and turned toward worldly things. In order to regain this awareness of God one must accept the Mediator, Jesus Christ (doctrine of Incarnation). One's will remains prideful if one does not accept the doctrine of Incarnation.[28]

A prideful will, then, is described as one in which the inclination

[27] Cushman, *op. cit.*, p. 288.
[28] *Ibid.*, p. 289.

towards God and the awareness of God are diminished. The *Imago Dei* is "obscured" or "defaced," as Cushman[29] puts it—diminished, obscured, or defaced from a previous condition in which awareness of God was at a high peak. Now, the problem for the philosopher is that of ascertaining criteria for the phrases "awareness of God" and "nonawareness of God" in order to understand the notion of a "prideful will" and hence the need for "faith preceding reason." The phrase "awareness of God" appears to describe a condition of man. But if this phrase is descriptive, what are the criteria for identifying a man who has this characteristic from one who does not? Are there any tests?

Cushman implicitly suggests that we can tell the difference by discovering if a man's will is "directed toward the creatures" or toward the "world of the senses." But these vague phrases are of no help at all. All of us in our daily intercourse must be "directed toward the creatures" or toward the "world of the senses" in some sense of those phrases. Perhaps the test suggested is "excessive direction toward the creatures or the world of the senses." But now the test is not one involving merely a description of a characteristic but a normative or moral judgment as well. Furthermore, in some senses of the phrase "directed toward the world of the senses" it could be that one is *not* so directed, and yet at the same time that one has *no* "awareness of or inclination towards God."

Some reasonably accurate test of the phrase "awareness of God" must be given if one is to understand the notion of a "prideful will," for such a will is defined as one which lacks (or has only slight) awareness of God. And the Augustinian contention that "faith must precede reason" is itself based on the supposition that a prideful will prevents genuine knowledge. Faith (acceptance of Christ or the doctrine of Incarnation) cleanses the prideful will, apparently makes one aware of God or restores the *Imago Dei,* and provides the proper point of reference for the correct interpretation of the data presented to man in the natural world. This, I think, is what Augustine is getting at when he declares that "faith must precede reason." But what is meant by this "awareness of God"? And assuming that this phrase is given some sort of determinate meaning, why must we

[29] *Ibid.,* p. 280.

assume that it provides the only correct point of reference for a correct interpretation of the data presented to man in the natural world?

In regard to the first of these two questions, no determinate meaning is given to the notion of "awareness of God." In fact, the issue of giving meaning to this phrase gives rise to the problem of the cognitive significance of the concept of God and of statements purportedly about God. Concerning the second question, no justifying grounds are given for the assumption that faith is the proper frame of reference for interpreting the data (certain historical events) presented to man in the natural world. If this is the case, the Augustinian dictum that "faith must precede reason" really amounts to the dogmatic assertion of a particular religious position. It differs radically from the kind of point made by David Hume—that before reason or science can operate, certain general assumptions must be made (the existence of the external world, cause and effect relationship, and induction) which themselves are presupposed, not proven. Augustine is suggesting that only if we adopt a certain religious position can our reason operate properly. But does reason really have a role, since the faith standpoint cannot be falsified by any data? For this reason we earlier suggested that there is no clear-cut distinction between faith and reason for the Augustinian, and it may well be the case that the Augustinian is left in the position of maintaining that faith is both a necessary and sufficient condition for knowledge—a most peculiar position indeed, a position which promotes complete fanaticism concerning beliefs.

Aside from the above problems, it seems to me that in a sense the Augustinian completely misses the most important point of the philosopher's question. The philosopher recognizes that the question of the meaning or cognitive significance of a statement is logically prior to the question of either the truth or falsity or the knowledge-status of that statement. Until one is reasonably clear about what is being claimed, one cannot possibly know what data are *relevant* to the confirmation or disconfirmation of the claim or if the data *are* confirming or disconfirming. Applying this point to the area of religion, the philosopher is maintaining that the question of the meaning or cognitive significance of a religious claim is a logically prior question to that of whether the claim is to be accepted on either faith or proof. The appeal to faith completely misses one very important point of the philosopher's question. The philosopher is really asking what he is supposed to have faith in—what is the meaning of the belief he is supposed to accept. To be sure, the Augustinian maintains that faith is not merely the acceptance of a group of propositions. The concept of faith is very complex as has been shown in several recent analyses.[30] But faith certainly does involve the acceptance of a proposition or set of propositions, even if it also involves other things. The philosopher's point, a point neglected by the Augustinian, is that you cannot justifiably ask or suggest that someone accept or believe a proposition or group of propositions unless it is made reasonably clear what the proposition, or set of propositions, means. If the religious claim has no clear meaning, can we even correctly speak of it as a proposition which can be accepted?

Let us take an example from the Augustinian position itself. Augustine maintains that acceptance of Christ as the son of God puts one in the proper frame of reference so that reason can function and genuine knowledge can be attained. We have seen, however, in connection with Brunner and Kierkegaard, that one interpretation of the doctrine of Incarnation is that it is "essentially paradoxical" or is an "absolute paradox"—meaning by this that it involves a logical contradiction. We have also noted that sentences which violate the principle of contradiction violate a fundamental requirement for the intelligible and informative use of language. This being the case, we must draw the inference that the doctrine of Incarnation (on Brunner and Kierkegaard's interpretation) has no cognitive significance, although it may have a great deal of emotive meaning. But yet we are urged to accept it or to believe it. Now how can one believe a sentence which has no content? The whole issue of the acceptance of such a sentence on faith or even proving it to be true cannot possibly arise, for no assertion is made in a genuine logical contradiction.

Now we would leave open the possibility of a formulation of the doctrine of Incarnation so that it is not paradoxical in Brunner's

[30] See John Hick, *op. cit.* and Paul Tillich, *Systematic Theology,* Vol. II (Chicago: Chicago University Press, 1957).

and Kierkegaard's sense of "paradoxical," although we are not aware of such a formulation which is satisfactory. But the example should make our point clear. The same issue would arise, for example, in connection with the notion of having an "awareness of God" or the notion of "being inclined toward God." Some determinate meaning must be given these phrases if they are to function informatively in sentences.

Our conclusion concerning the Augustinian approach to religious knowledge is that the "faith must precede reason" doctrine amounts to setting up either religious experience or faith as a necessary and sufficient condition for knowledge. This being the case, religious sentences based on either of these appeals do not constitute knowledge, for neither appeal gives one the right to be sure of the proposition believed or the claim based on that appeal. In fact, the appeal to faith or subjective certainty promotes complete fanaticism concerning beliefs. Even if beliefs based on faith or the feeling of psychological certainty happen to be true, we could still not classify them as knowledge.

(b) Similar objections hold against Kierkegaard's position, for his view that "truth is subjectivity" is very close to the Augustinian view. He remarks, for example, that "nature, the totality of created things, is the work of God. And yet God is not there; but within the individual man there is a potentiality (man is potentially spirit) which is awakened in inwardness to become a God-relationship, and then it becomes possible to see God everywhere."[31] Much like Augustine, Kierkegaard sets up faith, or what we would call subjective certainty, as a criterion for truth and knowledge. "It is subjectivity that Christianity is concerned with," he tells us," and it is only in subjectivity that its truth exists, if it exists at all; objectively Christianity has absolutely no existence."[32] That subjective certainty is his criterion is especially evident from his discussion of the notion of immortality. He asks, "When one man investigates objectively the problem of immortality, and another embraces an uncertainty with the passion of the infinite: where is there most

[31] Soren Kierkegaard, *Concluding Unscientific Postscript,* translated by David Swenson, completed and edited by Walter Lowrie (Princeton: Princeton University Press, 1941). Second Printing, 1944, pp. 220-221.

[32] *Ibid.,* p. 116.

truth, and who has the greater certainty? The one has entered upon a never-ending approximation, for the certainty of immortality lies precisely in the subjectivity of the individual." [33]

Now it is usually the case that a distinction is drawn between the two questions "Where is the most truth?" and "Who has the greater certainty?" One may have great certainty or feel psychologically certain of a belief and yet one's belief may be false or not constitute knowledge. It is not at all clear that Kierkegaard draws this distinction concerning religious knowledge. Referring to the feeling of psychological certainty that one's soul is immortal he asks, "Is any better proof capable of being given for the immortality of the soul?" Elsewhere he writes, "The conclusions of passion are the only reliable ones, that is, the only convincing ones." Although he implicitly distinguishes between objective and subjective certainty, Kierkegaard maintains that subjective certainty or faith (defined as "the highest passion in the sphere of human subjectivity") is a necessary and sufficient condition for *religious* knowledge. In regard to religious truth the principle of contradiction is "annulled" [34] and "truth becomes a paradox. The eternal truth has come into being in time: this is the paradox." [35] The paradox is the doctrine of Incarnation, but this doctrine constitutes religious knowledge if it is "held fast in the passion of inwardness."

Interpreting Kierkegaard in this manner it is clear that the same objections cited against Augustine's view hold against his. Faith is set up as a necessary and sufficient condition for religious knowledge. But faith, or the feeling of psychological certainty, does not give one the "right to be sure" of a given belief, and hence beliefs accepted solely on these grounds do not constitute knowledge. The appeal to subjective certainty alone promotes complete fanaticism concerning beliefs.

A further problem confronting Kierkegaard's position (which does not confront Augustine, I think) is that faith is to be recommended in proportion to the absurdity or paradoxicality of one's belief.[36] We have argued, however, that if a belief is actually absurd in

[33] *Ibid.*, p. 180.
[34] *Ibid.*, p. 181.
[35] *Ibid.*, p. 187.
[36] *Ibid.*

Kierkegaard's sense (violating the principle of contradiction) it can have no cognitive significance, for it violates a fundamental requirement for the intelligible and informative use of language. The issue of whether a religious "absurdity" or "paradox" is true or constitutes knowledge could not possibly arise. Augustine, on the other hand, does not maintain that faith recommends itself in proportion to the absurdity of the belief, or that religious beliefs are absurd in Kierkegaard's sense of "absurd." Such beliefs are "foolishness to the Greeks," but Augustine nowhere maintains that they are logical contradictions.

(c) Although I will not here attempt a detailed analysis, I believe that the principal objections which we have cited against Augustine and Kierkegaard also hold against the view of Paul Tillich, one of the most renowned Protestant theologians of our time. Tillich follows closely in the Augustinian tradition. In somewhat different language, he maintains that (1) "faith must precede reason," and (2) that man has "fallen" and lost in part his *Imago Dei*. ". . . it is the image of God in man which gives the possibility of the Fall. Only he who is the image of God has the power of separating himself from God." [37] The loss of the *Imago Dei* or "separation from God" Tillich calls "estrangement." Estrangement he characterizes as "unbelief" and "unfaith," a "state in which man in the totality of his being turns away from God. In his existential self-realization he turns toward himself and his world and loses his essential unity with the ground of his being and his world." [38] Unbelief or unfaith is a state in which there is a "separation of man's will from the will of God." Unbelief or estrangement is also characterized as a state of "concupiscence"—"the unlimited desire to draw the whole of reality into one's self. It refers to all aspects of man's relation to himself and to his world." [39]

As long as one is in a state of concupiscence and estrangement one can have no knowledge of God. Knowledge of God is *immediate* and is had through one's religious consciousness when the obstacle of concupiscence or estrangement is gone. Speaking of this approach as Augustinian, Tillich says of the Franciscan developers of this

[37] Paul Tillich, *Systematic Theology*, Vol. II (Chicago, 1957), p. 33.
[38] *Ibid.*, p. 47.
[39] *Ibid.*, p. 52.

position, "The Franciscan school of the 13th century . . . developed the Augustinian solution into a doctrine of the principles of theology and maintained the ontological type of the philosophy of religion. Their whole emphasis was on the immediacy of the knowledge of God. According to Bonaventura "God is most truly present to the very soul and is immediately knowable; he is knowable in himself and without media . . ." [40]

Now Tillich characterizes his own position in philosophy of religion as the "ontological way" or "ontological approach," and identifies himself with this tradition. The beginning point for religious knowledge is not the world or nature from which one *infers* the existence of God. The beginning point is the *self* or the religious consciousness, and there is in fact an avoidance of any inferential process. Emphasis is on *immediacy,* where apprehension, understanding, and acceptance are all one, and certainty comes, as Tillich says, "out of the things themselves without a medium." [41] Knowledge of God is a recovery of something one always dimly has had but which has become obscured, and this recovery is contingent upon the individual's will. One has knowledge of God when one has faith, faith being viewed not merely as the acceptance of certain propositions but as a condition of one's will, a condition in which estrangement is overcome.

It can easily be seen that Tillich's "ontological approach" is open to the same objections which we posed against Augustine. First, it is not clear what kind of thesis Tillich is arguing when he says that man is in a state of estrangement, or that man has lost his "essential unity with the ground of his being and his world." This is the same sort of claim as that of Augustine when he says that man's reason is disabled by sinful pride. We saw that it was not clear whether Augustine's thesis was normative or descriptive, and further that there were no clear-cut criteria for the application of the term "prideful will." This is also the case with Tillich's claim that man is in a state of estrangement, that man has lost his essential unity with the grounds of his being and his world, or that man's

[40] Paul Tillich, "The Two Types of Philosophy of Religion," *Union Seminary Quarterly Review,* no. 4 (May, 1946), p. 4.

[41] Quoted by John F. Smith, "The Present Status of Natural Theology," in *The Journal of Philosophy,* Vol. 55, no. 22 (October 23, 1958), p. 932.

will is separated from the will of God. Obviously until some clear meaning is given Professor Tillich's contention, one cannot evaluate its truth or falsity. Apparently the only evidence relevant to his contention is found in the self. One has the feeling or awareness of estrangement. Presumably, one is aware of both the meaning of his claim and of the evidence relevant to its truth in one's immediate experience.

This appeal to immediate awareness gives rise to our second major criticism of Professor Tillich's "ontological approach." Both the meaning and truth of the claim that man is estranged from God or that, on occasion, man is reunited with God and has knowledge of God are based, not on any inferences, but upon man's immediate awareness or intuition. Tillich assumes that these claims are not merely claims about the psychological states of persons, but that they also have objective import. They concern a relationship between man and God or "being-itself."

However, does this appeal to "immediate experience" of estrangement or reunion constitute sufficient evidence to justify a knowledge-claim, a claim that one is in fact estranged from or reunited with God or "being-itself"? We have argued that the appeal to "immediate experience" or intuition is not a generally reliable appeal and hence does not give one the right to be sure of a claim which has objective import. The fact that one has an experience does not insure that it is veridical. Such a claim then cannot be said to constitute knowledge. But a logically prior and even more important problem confronting Tillich's position is that of setting forth the meaning of the claim that man is estranged or has lost his essential unity with the ground of his being. (We commented in some detail in an earlier chapter on the difficulties involved in Tillich's appeal to "symbolic" meaning and truth.) Some maintain that these phrases convey no meaning to them. Others maintain that they understand at least in part what Tillich is claiming, but deny that they have the experience of estrangement at all. Surely maintaining that these people are blind is begging the question. Those who do not have the experience of estrangement can as justly argue that those who have the experience are having hallucinations. Tillich himself recognizes that naturalistic philosophers deny that there is estrangement or a "human predicament." All that Tillich has to say of the naturalist is, "If the idealist or naturalist asserts that 'there is no human predicament,' he makes an existential decision about a matter of ultimate concern . . . The philosopher cannot avoid existential decisions. . . ." [42] Tillich does not say that the naturalist is wrong. He maintains that each person must make his own existential decision on this matter. Implicitly, however, Tillich does contend that the naturalist is wrong and that the existential decision of the Christian is the appropriate one. It is appropriate because man is *really* estranged. But let me repeat, the evidence for this claim is immediate experience or intuition, and surely such a claim cannot be classified as knowledge even if it happens to be true.

Historical Religious Claims

"Christ lived and worked in Nazareth," "Christ was crucified and raised from the dead," "Mohammed had a prophetic call and undertook a ministry in Mecca"—these and many other religious sentences are taken to be historical truths. In fact, the entire biblical story has been taken to be an accurate chronicle of history. Many contemporary biblical scholars, however, no longer accept a literal interpretation of many of these so-called historical truths. The account of the Creation, the Fall, and the Last Coming, the view of Heaven and Hell, the doctrine of the Virgin Birth, the miracles of Jesus, the Resurrection and Ascension, and the Atonement—all these are taken to be part of a mythological picture by Professor Rudolf Bultmann and other theologians.[43] The stories of the Gospel, Bultmann argues, must be "demythologized" if they are to be accepted as meaningful in a scientific age. The problem is that of specifying which religious claims about history are to be taken as literal, factual claims and which as myths. Assuming that there are testing criteria and methodological procedures for deciding this, there is still the problem of whether religious claims constitute knowledge. If a given religious sentence or belief is declared a myth, then it

[42] Paul Tillich, *Systematic Theology,* Vol. II, p. 30.

[43] Rudolf Bultmann, *Jesus Christ and Mythology* (New York: Charles Scribner's Sons, 1958), and his essay in *Kerygma and Myth,* edited by H. W. Bartsch, translated by R. H. Fuller (New York: Harper & Row, Publishers, 1961).

logically follows that one cannot speak of it as being true in any literal sense. However, many will claim of religious myths that they are symbolically true or analogically true. We will not repeat the difficulties attending the appeal to symbolic and analogical meaning and truth.[44] If a given religious sentence or belief is declared to be a *literal* historical truth, then that belief must be treated by reference to our specified criteria for knowledge. We think there are a number of historical claims which fulfill the function we denominated as religious and which have considerable evidence in their favor—archeological evidence, recorded testimony, etc.,—and which merit some degree of belief. For example, the claim that Christ was crucified is reasonably well documented by written testimony and historical data. There are a number of eye-witness accounts of this occurrence, and we have no reason for assuming that all these accounts were biased or that all the witnesses were having hallucinations. The claim merits a high degree of belief given the amount of data which supports it, and can be characterized as knowledge. Other historical claims which perform a religious function and which are designed to be taken as literal truths may not have enough evidence in their favor to merit belief. For example, the belief that Christ rose from the dead is often set forth as a literal truth. But what data are there which support this belief? We have no eye-witness accounts. The documents we do have were written several decades after the alleged event.[45] Furthermore, it is significant that there are few or no claims of persons rising from the dead in more recent centuries, centuries in which more evidence and accuracy has been demanded of writers. In the light of these facts, many maintain that the proposition that Christ literally rose from the dead does not merit belief.

The religious claim that history documents the existence of miracles, and hence the existence of a God responsible for those miracles, deserves special mention. Bultmann suggests that the miracles of Christ be viewed as part of a mythological picture. When miracles are viewed this way, the question of their literal truth does not arise. Others, however, insist that the miracles of Christ

[44] See Chapter Five above.

[45] Paul Tillich, *op. cit.*, p. 155; and H. J. Paton, *The Modern Predicament* (London, 1955), p. 237.

(and other miracles) are to be taken as literally true. When this is the case a number of problems arise which we will mention but not discuss in detail. First, there is the problem of specifying the meaning of "miracle." The word is often used in a number of ways. A miracle, however, is generally interpreted by the religious as an intervention of the supernatural or God in nature which does not conform to any natural law and which results in a temporary suspension of natural law. If he accepts this definition of a miracle, the religious advocate must provide evidence that there is a God or a supernatural order which can and does impinge upon the natural order of events. Then he must show that a given event is such an impingement. We submit that neither of these has been done. Obviously, there are many events which defy explanation within the framework of known natural law. But the assertion that they are the result of God's intervention is not justified. There may be natural laws of which we are as yet unaware. So-called miracles may some day be shown to conform to natural laws which are now unknown. Even if an unusual event did not ever conform to any natural law, this would only show that this event was undetermined. This is the thesis of many nonreligious indeterminists, namely, that many events are not the result of a cause-and-effect, deterministic scheme. The inference that such events are intervening acts of God does not follow.

Ignoring for the moment the need to show that there must be an intervening God in order for a miracle to take place (indeed this is tautological), there is the further problem of showing that the unusual events claimed to be miraculous occurred at all. David Hume has argued that, in the case of *most* of these unusual events, there is not sufficient reliable evidence (from witnesses, testimony, and memory) to make the belief that these unusual events occurred reasonable.[46] We agree with Hume on this point. In cases where there is considerable evidence for the occurrence of an unusual event, the problem then becomes the justification of interpreting the event as a miracle. When these unusual events are interpreted as

[46] David Hume, "Of Miracles," in *Enquiries Concerning the Human Understanding and Concerning the Principles of Morals*; reprinted from the original and edited by L. A. Selby-Bigge (Oxford: Clarendon Press, impression of 1951). Second edition published in 1962.

miracles, Hume's insistence upon empirical evidence sufficient to render the occurrence of such events probable has the effect of ruling out a priori that belief in a miracle could ever be credible; for a miracle is *defined* as being *improbable.* Hume does not, however, rule out the *possibility* that these unusual events did occur, and that they are acts of God. The problem is that the interpretation of these unusual events (assuming that they occurred) as acts of God is not justified; for the "theistic hypothesis," as Hume puts it, is itself unjustified.

The Classical Arguments for God's Existence: Teleological, Cosmological, and Ontological

Thus far we have examined the appeals to religious experience, mystical experience, revelation, faith, historical events, and miracles as grounds for the truth of certain religious sentences. A number of natural theologians, however, appeal to a different kind of evidence, especially for the truth of the existence of God. They maintain that God's existence is an empirical hypothesis, and that belief in God is justified, just as is any other hypothesis, by reference to empirical data. God's existence cannot be logically demonstrated, but it can be shown that it is a reasonable inference from empirical data. As F. R. Tennant puts it, "Natural theology sets out from facts and inductions; its premises are as firmly established and as universally acknowledged as any of the stable generalizations of science." [47] And again, "The empirically minded theologian . . . would let the actual world tell its own story and offer its own suggestions; not silence it while abstractive speculation . . . weaves a system of thought which may prove to conflict with facts." [48]

The empirical evidence cited by Tennant and others is generally subsumed under what is called the teleological argument. Hume in his *Dialogues* called this the argument from design, for it is an argument from the existence of design and purpose in the world to the existence of a cosmic Designer or Purposer. That this argument is confronted by a number of problems has been shown by

[47] F. R. Tennant, *Philosophical Theology,* Vol. II (Cambridge, 1928-30), p. 79.
[48] *Ibid.,* p. 78.

many philosophers. Not the least of these problems is that of specifying the exact nature of the hypothesis to be confirmed, namely, the nature of the God which the evidence of design is to establish. Is God to be viewed as both omnipotent and perfectly good? And are the meanings of the terms "power" and "goodness" to be interpreted as they are in human contexts? Or are the meanings of these terms when applied to God beyond our comprehension, as many theologians argue? And if they are beyond our comprehension, can we possibly know what hypothesis we are trying to confirm? If the design hypothesis is taken to imply a God who is omnipotent and perfectly good, and the terms "power" and "goodness" are to mean what they ordinarily mean, then the hypothesis has some clear meaning. However, the evidence points to at least as much evil and suffering in the world as there is good. In other words, there is considerable empirical evidence (which we will not here describe) against this hypothesis; and there is even evidence which supports the hypothesis that God, though perhaps omnipotent, is evil and wants living things to suffer.

Theologians who employ the teleological argument have, of course, devised a number of means to avoid attributing evil to God. We have mentioned one of those devices, namely, the view that the goodness of God is incomprehensible. Another is that God is completely good but not all-powerful, there being an evil power in the universe. Still another device is that of maintaining that evil is only "apparent." Events appear to be evil because of our human perspective, but if we could see things in the long run—even from the point of view of eternity—we would see that what appears to be evil is really good, and that God is completely good.

However, these devices (and others which we will not consider) appear inadequate. The first leaves the design hypothesis without any clear meaning. One could not possibly discover whether any given evidence was confirming or disconfirming. The second leaves the hypothesis with clear meaning, but commits the theologian to metaphysical dualism, a position most theologians wish to avoid because it leaves the outcome of the world contingent—the evil power, God's adversary, may well win the struggle. The third is inadequate, because the same logic supports the opposite conclusion. One might argue that the good in the world is only "apparent," and if we could see things in the long run—from an infinite perspective—we would see that what appears to be good is really evil, and that God is completely evil.

The design hypothesis is also involved in other problems. David Hume has pointed out that the argument is an argument from analogy. A given feature of the empirical world is taken as a basis for the analogy, and one extrapolates that there is a divine Designer responsible for that feature. William Paley gives as an example that if we discovered a watch in the middle of a desert, we would infer that there was a watchmaker. In the same way we may infer from the existence of the universe and its various features that there is a universe-maker. The problems surrounding Paley's analogy have often been pointed out. There is very little similarity between a watch and a universe. Furthermore, in the case of watches and watch-makers we have direct observational evidence, whereas in the case of the universe and a universe-maker there is no such evidence. His argument from analogy moves illegitimately from watch-maker and watch, something within our experience, to universe-maker, something totally outside our experience. This is really an indictment of the logic of any argument from analogy which attempts to draw inferences about something completely outside experience. To justify the position that the order in the universe is the result of a Designer, we must have observational data showing that that order proceeds from a Designer. For this reason the design argument *proves* nothing, although the possibility of such a Designer is not thereby ruled out.

Even if the design argument from analogy were logically adequate, there would remain the problem of what we could know about this unobserved Designer. Often it is inferred that the existence of intelligence, adaptation, and goodness in the world shows that the Designer is intelligent and good. However, as Hume so clearly points out, there are other features of the universe besides intelligence and goodness. One is the existence of plant and vegetable life and living organisms. Are we not as justified in inferring from the argument from analogy that, like a plant or a living organism, the universe is the result of "generation" or "vegetation," not of design? Hume's own view is that if the argument from analogy proves one conclusion it equally well proves another—but the argument from analogy really proves nothing at all.

If the design hypothesis is interpreted not as a thesis about an unobservable Designer but simply as the thesis that there is order and value in the universe, then we must grant that such a thesis is supported by much empirical evidence. However, the design argument is almost always taken as proving the existence of an unobserved and unobservable Deity. Theological operationalists like H. N. Wieman do in fact identify the *meaning* of the term "God" with "creative value" and order.[49] If the design hypothesis were interpreted along Wieman's operational lines simply as the hypothesis that there is value and order in the world, then certainly it is cognitively meaningful since it is confirmed to a large extent. Exactly in what manner Wieman's position on religion differs from philosophical naturalism, however, is difficult to discern.

In spite of the difficulties confronting confirmation of the design hypothesis, in most cases it is clearly a cognitively meaningful hypothesis, since it has some clear meaning and there is some empirical evidence relevant to its confirmation. On some occasions, however, the thesis that a Designer or God exists, especially a God with characteristics like "absolute goodness" and "absolute power," is qualified, when questioned and analyzed, in such a manner that it is made compatible with any state of affairs whatever. Flew has shown how this is done in the case of the sentence "God loves us as a father loves his children." The thesis that a Designer or God exists can be similarly qualified so that no evidence will count as falsifying evidence. We have already noted that when this occurs the question of whether the sentence or hypothesis is cognitively meaningful arises. What clear meaning can a hypothesis have which is compatible with any empirical state of affairs and incompatible with none?

Aside from the design argument, there are the other traditional arguments for God's existence—the cosmological and ontological arguments. The objections to these arguments are well known. The

[49] H. N. Wieman and W. M. Horton, *The Growth of Religion* (Chicago, 1938); and H. N. Wieman, "Can God Be Perceived?" in *Journal of Religion,* Vol. 23 (1943).

cosmological argument rests on the supposition that nothing can exist or occur without a sufficient cause, and then maintains that God is the sufficient cause of everything. Aside from the question of whether the thesis of causal determinism upon which this argument rests is itself valid, it is clear that the cosmological argument is an inconsistent application of the principle of determinism. It is inconsistent to maintain that every effect has a cause, and that there is a First Cause or Uncaused Cause. Furthermore, it is perfectly conceivable that time has no beginning, and that every event was preceded by an earlier event. Even assuming that the argument established the existence of a First Cause, it does not establish anything whatever concerning the characteristics, moral and other, of the First Cause. It does not establish the existence of the *kind* of God that those who employ the argument are interested in establishing.

The ontological argument attempts to move from the supposed fact that we have an idea of a completely perfect Being to the actual existence of that perfect Being—on the grounds that existence is necessary to perfection. Again the objections to this argument are well known. There is the initial problem of the meaning of the phrase "perfect Being." We have seen that predicates like "perfect" when applied to God are often said not to mean what they mean in ordinary contexts. There is a serious problem of specifying this nonliteral meaning of "perfect." In ordinary contexts, when we say that something is perfect we generally mean perfect for some end or goal, but those who employ the ontological argument simply say that God is perfect without specifying in what way. Furthermore, there seem to be a number of different conceptions of God or this "perfect Being," so if the argument is valid it really proves the existence of a number of Gods. The ontological argument also fails for other reasons. It assumes that "existence" is a predicate or a property like "blue" or "green." It has been pointed out by philosophers that, although sentences like "Tables exist" and "Tables are brown" are grammatically similar, they are logically different. This logical difference is evident when "existence" is treated as a predicate like "brown," for then all positive existential statements become tautologies, and all negative existential statements become self-contradictory. Hospers makes the point by using the example,

" 'Horses are herbivorous' means 'If there is (exists) anything that is a horse, then it is herbivorous.' On this analysis, 'Horses exist' would become 'If there exists anything that is a horse, then it exists,' which is a flat tautology and is obviously not what the statement means at all. Moreover, 'Horses do not exist' would become 'If horses exist, then horses do not exist,' which is an outright self-contradiction, whereas the original statement is merely false." [50]

That existence is not a predicate is sometimes shown by pointing out that the notion of existence adds nothing to the concept of a thing. As Kant puts it, "By whatever and by however many predicates we may think a thing . . . we do not make the least addition to the thing when we further declare that this thing is." [51] If Kant is correct, and existence is not part of the concept of a thing, then it is clear that the ontological argument which attempts to deduce the existence of God from the concept of God is fallacious.

There is yet a further difficulty which confronts the ontological argument. It is clear that even if the assumption that existence is a predicate or is included in the concept of perfection is permitted, this does not prove that that perfect thing exists. All that is shown is that if one is to have a correct concept of that perfect being, he must *think* of it as existing. But the concept of a perfect being's existing does not entail the actual existence of that perfect being.[52]

[50] See John Hospers, *An Introduction to Philosophical Analysis* (Englewood Cliffs, N. J.: Prentice-Hall, Inc., 1953), p. 326.

[51] Immanuel Kant, *Critique of Pure Reason,* Norman Kemp-Smith translation, (New York: Humanities Press, 1950), pp. 505-506.

[52] For contemporary reassessments of the ontological argument, see Norman Malcolm's "Anselm's Ontological Arguments," in *The Philosophical Review,* vol. 69 (1960); R. E. Allen's "The Ontological Argument," Raziel Abelson's "Not Necessarily," Terence Penelhum's "On the Second Ontological Argument," Alvin Plantinga's "A Valid Ontological Argument?," Paul Henle's "Uses of the Ontological Argument" and Gareth Matthews' "On Conceivability in Anselm and Malcolm"—all in *The Philosophical Review,* vol. 70 (January, 1961).

CHAPTER NINE

Conclusion

We have examined a number of different types of evidence adduced for the truth of various religious utterances. The appeals to religious experience, mystical experience, revelation, historical occurrences, and miracles have been examined. We have analyzed the Augustinian approach to religious knowledge, and the traditional rational arguments for God's existence.

Sentences which perform a religious function, we have suggested, are of many different kinds. They include descriptions, predictions, explanations, exclamations, exhortations, prayers, questions, ejaculations, blessings, historical statements, and autobiographical statements. There are also sentences, we have seen, which purport to refer to something outside human experience—something in principle unverifiable. And there are other religious sentences to which no falsifying evidence is permitted. Adequate philosophical analysis requires that each kind of religious sentence which purports to be true be examined and classified. This will enable one to discover what sort of evidence, if any, is relevant to the confirmation of the sentence, and to ascertain whether it conforms to the criteria for knowledge.

We have suggested that many cognitive religious sentences (for example, "Christ lived in Nazareth," "Christ was crucified," "Mohammed engaged in a ministry in Mecca") have a great deal of evidence relevant to their confirmation. They merit *some degree* of the attitude of belief and to that extent constitute justified knowledge claims. Other religious claims (that certain miracles occurred; that Christ literally rose from the dead; that the Red Sea parted, permitting Moses and the Israelites to cross, and then closed, drowning the Egyptians; that a given drought was caused by sinfulness, etc.) do not have enough evidence supporting them to merit one's belief, and hence are not justified knowledge-claims.

The religious sentences which provide the biggest problem to one asking if there is religious knowledge, however, are those which claim to impart knowledge but to which no falsifying evidence applies or which must be taken as analogically or symbolically true. Often included in this group are "God created the world," "God is a loving heavenly father," "Christ is the son of God," "God is triune," "God is angry at sin," "The Holy Spirit descended upon them," and "Christ rose from the dead." It is sentences of this kind, rather than ordinary descriptive, historical, or explanatory sentences designed to be taken literally, which constitute the core of those sentences fulfilling the function we have described as religious, the function of providing a focal attitude of orientation and object or objects of devotion. We have argued that any statement can be said to constitute a justified knowledge claim if it has some clear meaning, and if there is sufficient evidence supporting it. But we have further argued that the appeal to the so-called analogical or symbolical (as opposed to literal) function of these key religious sentences does not help us to discover their meaning. The problem, then, with such sentences is not so much whether they constitute knowledge, but whether they say anything which can be true or false, i.e., whether they are cognitively meaningful. If these sentences cannot be interpreted so that they conform to our criteria for cognitivity, it analytically follows that they do not constitute knowledge. The question of according any of these sentences some degree of the attitude of belief cannot even arise unless they are given some clear meaning.

We have concluded that certain key religious sentences—when interpreted as being "analogically true" or "symbolically true," or when interpreted as purporting to refer to an unobserved and unobservable object though they cannot possibly be falsified by any data—not only do not constitute knowledge, but are also not cognitively meaningful. This conclusion does not imply that those beliefs or attitudes have no value in the lives of people. Nor are we suggesting that religious beliefs and attitudes should be given up.

Both the cognitive status and the knowledge status of a belief are at least partially independent of the psychological and pragmatic import of a belief.

Our conclusions concerning the cognitive status and knowledge status of religious beliefs rest upon the acceptance of two norms, a norm which functions as a criterion for cognitivity, and a norm which functions as a criterion for knowledge. Max Black, Rudolf Carnap, Herbert Feigl, and other philosophers have shown that the justification of something requires showing that it is consistent with, or deducible from, a standard. And showing that something is not justified requires showing that it is inconsistent with a standard. To discover whether or not a given sentence, religious or otherwise, constitutes knowledge or is a sound belief one must discover whether that sentence or belief conforms to a standard or criterion for knowledge. Whether there is religious knowledge cannot possibly be discussed until criteria for the term "knowledge" have been provided. Once such criteria have been provided, or once we are provided with a set of rules governing belief, then and only then can the question "Is there religious knowledge?" be sensibly asked and answered. The question is answered by seeing if religious sentences which purport to be true conform to the standard or norm for knowledge. The question "Is there religious knowledge?" is not a straightforward factual question like "Is salt soluble?" The normative question "What criteria for the term 'knowledge' ought we to adopt?" must first be answered. In the last analysis, the clash between those who maintain that the key religious sentences mentioned above do constitute knowledge and those who deny this is based upon *normative differences.* They differ on both the norm or standard for cognitivity and the norm or standard for knowledge.

The conclusions drawn in this book, then, can certainly be rejected by simply rejecting the premises (the account of cognitive meaning and the criteria for knowledge) from which the conclusions were drawn. However, should those premises be rejected, the burden of providing and justifying an alternative account of cognitive meaning and an alternative set of criteria for knowledge must be assumed. And it must then be shown that religious beliefs conform to these standards.

Suppose that disagreement over whether there is religious knowledge is rooted in the acceptance of different norms—different accounts of cognitive meaning and different criteria for knowledge. Can this disagreement be rationally settled? Some logical positivists maintain that it cannot. All norms are emotive or noncognitive, and only persuasive reasons, not justifying ones can be cited in their behalf. To some extent, we think, the positivist is correct, and that extent can be set forth by referring to a distinction formulated by Herbert Feigl,[1] a distinction between validation (*justificatia cognitionis*) and vindication (*justificatia actionis*).

For Feigl, the justifying principles (norms) in validation are the rules of deductive and inductive inference. Any knowledge-claim must ultimately make reference to those rules. On the other hand, purposes, together with empirical knowledge of means-ends relations, serve as the basis for vindication or pragmatic justification. When justifying principles serve as the basis for validation, there can be no appeal to other, more ultimate grounds of validation without vicious circularity. As Feigl puts it, "Validation terminates with the exhibition of the norms that govern the realm of argument concerned. If any further question can be raised at all, it must be the question concerning the pragmatic justification (vindication) of the (act of) adoption of the validating principles." [2]

Feigl's distinction is specifically applicable to the argument of this book. In our argument we adopted certain criteria for the correct use of the term "knowledge." Those criteria (which include reliance upon the methodological procedures of deductive and inductive logic) serve as our ultimate validating appeal. In asking if any given religious proposition constituted knowledge we appealed to these criteria, but we did not question the criteria themselves. Now those criteria can surely be questioned. If they are questioned we cannot prove them or validate them by reference to any other standard without vicious circularity. We can only offer vindicating reasons for adopting those criteria. And all that vindication does is to make

[1] Herbert Feigl, "Validation and Vindication: An Analysis of the Nature and Limits of Ethical Arguments," in *Readings in Ethical Theory,* edited by Wilfred Sellars and John Hospers (New York: © 1952 by Appleton-Century Crofts, Inc.), p. 674. A revised version of an earlier essay, "De Principii Non Disputandum . . . ?" in *Philosophical Analysis,* edited by Max Black (Ithaca, N. Y.: Cornell University Press, 1950).

[2] *Ibid.,* p. 675.

clear which aims or goals are attained by the adoption of given validating principles. In the case of adopting certain criteria for the term "knowledge," vindication can only point out the results (considered to be good or desirable) which accrue from the adoption of those criteria. We indicated earlier the vindicating grounds or the results (which we consider good and desirable) which accrue from adopting our proposed criteria and methods for knowledge. Once these criteria and methods are adopted, we have a way of distinguishing credible knowledge claims from those which are not, and, consequently, a means of solving what we take to be the central problem of epistemology, namely, what degree of belief one should accord to cognitive sentences of various kinds. Furthermore, the use of these criteria yields a body of logically consistent beliefs and offers the advantage of intersubjective agreement on the propositions tested. Other implicitly accepted criteria for knowledge (such as the appeal to "religious experience," revelation, intuition, "faith") cannot provide these desirable results, and in fact tend to promote complete fanaticism concerning beliefs. For one who does not find these results desirable (and our formulation of the central problem of epistemology acceptable), these reasons will not vindicate or pragmatically justify these criteria for the term "knowledge." Vindicating reasons are not logically coercive. They are reasons intended to persuade, and whether or not they are efficacious depends upon whether those reasons conform to one's interests, purposes, or ideals.

The goals or desired results of the majority of the believers of the world's religions, it seems to me, are something other than mere concern for truth or consistency. The religions of the world abound in internal inconsistencies which are simply ignored by advocates of those religions.[3] Furthermore, in cases in which religious claims have some clear meaning, certain of these claims either lack evidence or are confronted with considerable disconfirming evidence. This, however, does not inhibit the believing attitude of the religious person, for most religious persons do not treat religious propositions as hypotheses which are to be subject to impartial inquiry and testing. We have noted that in many cases the believer actually will permit no possible data to be considered as falsifying what he

[3] See Joseph Margolis, "What is Religious Truth?" *Review of Religion*, 20 (November, 1955), 39.

believes, and sometimes he insists (and admits that he does so) upon believing the irrational—that which is contrary to a rational relief. These facts indicate to me that the goal of a religion is often something other than concern for truth or consistency, namely, the fulfillment of certain of man's psychic needs. A religion, we have argued, provides one with a focal attitude of orientation and an object or objects of devotion and, in doing so, it fulfills certain of man's psychic needs. The fulfillment of these needs is the desired result, and any evidence or belief tending to undercut the beliefs which provide that focal attitude of orientation and object of devotion are undesirable. This is why the criteria we have suggested for knowledge are unacceptable to many religious persons. Acceptance of those criteria would endanger beliefs central to the given frame of orientation of a religion, and would be considered detrimental to the desired goal of persons operating in that religion. Since the persuasive efficacy of vindicating reasons depends upon what goals, interests, or ideas are accepted, and since the desired goals and ideals of two parties are often different, then it is obvious that vindicating reasons for each party will differ. When this occurs, there can be no *pragmatic* resolvement of the disagreements between the two parties—much less a *rational* resolvement. This, it seems to me, is the present state of affairs, and the perennial state of affairs, between many religious advocates and other parties—including some scientists, positivists, and empiricists. The desiderata of these groups differ. This means that acceptable vindicating reasons for each party differ, and since vindicating reasons are the only reasons which can be given once an ultimate validating appeal is made, then we are left with groups with different attitudes toward life, different goals and ideals. We terminate this book on the question "Is there religious knowledge?" by recognizing this fact, a fact best stated by Nietzsche in the *Antichrist* when he said that for some people "it is a matter of complete indifference whether something is true, while it is of the utmost importance whether it is believed to be true. Truth and faith that something is true: two completely separate realms of interest—almost diametrically opposite realms—they are reached by utterly different paths."

Index